A Place in the Sun

A Place in the Sun
David E. Lovewell

Text © 2014 David E. Lovewell

All rights reserved. No portion of this book may be copied or distributed without the express written consent of the author or (in the case of illustrations) illustrator, with the exception of "fair use" quotation in other works of not more than eight lines from any given poem.

ISBN 978-1-312-64858-6

A Place in the Sun

To *the memory of my parents,*
Gladys and Ernest Lovewell,
without whom there would have been no place in the sun.

David E. Lovewell

A Place in the Sun

Contents

Foreword	*ix*
Chapter 1: Shotesham Lad	*1*
Chapter 2: Early School Days	*15*
Chapter 3: The War Years	*28*
Chapter 4: New Horizons	*54*
Chapter 5: Canada Bound	*70*
Chapter 6: My Final Sermon	*91*
Chapter 7: Re-Creation	*96*

David E. Lovewell

Foreword

I originally wrote these memoirs of my early life for my own benefit. I offer them to others who have a connection with that long-ago time or who have come to know me over the years. Because of my penchant for reminiscence, most family and friends will have heard some of the tales I relate here. I trust it helps to have those stories placed in context. What I've written also says as much about me now as it does about me in my formative days. Recapturing the past is impossible, I realize, so my goal is more modest: to evoke the wonder I feel when, across the chasm of decades, I revisit a time that seems as fresh as yesterday. If I manage to impart some of that wonder, I will feel happy to have succeeded.

David E. Lovewell

A Place in the Sun

Chapter 1: Shotesham Lad

To a casual passerby, the village I grew up in seems timeless. A winding line of mostly wattle and daub cottages and houses, interspersed with fields and dominated by an ancient flint-stoned church tower, it holds about the same number of people—500 or so souls—as it has for the past millennium. So it comes by its timelessness honestly. Its origins are associated with a small stream known as the Beck which runs through the meadow behind what was once my family's home at Grove Farm. My brother Ivan, sister Beryl and I would play there as children. In winter it could be a raging torrent, whose dangers were severely impressed on us. In summer, when it was sometimes little more than a trickle, especially during hot spells, we would make dams and fish for tiddlers and gudgeons.

During Roman times the Beck was navigable for about another mile beyond our house. As an adult Ivan farmed the fields at that spot. He uncovered pottery shards, Roman coins and weights—evidence of exchange between the Romans and the local Iceni. This trading post was connected to the river system in the vicinity, as vessels from the coastal Roman fort at Caister-on-Sea followed the rivers Yare and Tas and then as far up as they could manage on the Beck.

That meant that the place now known as Shotesham wasn't exactly off the civilized map two thousand years ago. But for many centuries after that it might as well have been. At some point the Beck became unnavigable. Once the Romans had left and the Saxons and Angles arrived in their stead, the village may have glimpsed Queen Boadicea's army or Viking marauders but through all that time it must have been little more than an isolated

Portrait of Frances, Countess of Surrey, by Hans Holbein the Younger. Royal Collection, Windsor Castle.

peasant habitation. By the time of William the Conqueror's Domesday Book it was an identifiable hamlet divided into twelve "scots" or sections from whence it took its name, but its quiet pastoral life continued, only rarely marked by events noticed elsewhere.

As it happened, our own farmhouse is said to have played a role in one such event. A noblewoman named Frances Howard, wife of the Earl of Surrey and great granddaughter of the John de Vere who appears in two of Shakespeare's history plays, was passing through the village in February 1539 when she went into labour. Villagers have long believed that the dwelling where she stopped was Grove Farm.

Her son, Henry Howard, would not forget his birth in Shotesham. A courtier during the reigns of Elizabeth and James I, he was a scholarly sort often described in history books as an intriguer. He was also a bachelor who amassed considerable wealth during his lifetime.[1] At his death, he endowed three alms houses in different

---

1 Much of this wealth derived from the lucrative positions Howard gained under James I - indeed, as I write in 2014 new evidence is coming to light concerning secret political correspondence he seems to have had with James before the latter's accession to the English throne. During James's reign he was given the title Earl of Northampton and made Lord Warden of the Cinque Ports. He is probably best remembered today for the high-stakes political quarrel he waged with his maternal cousin Edward de Vere, the 17th Earl of Oxford, inspiration of today's thriving Oxfordian movement whose adherents believe that de Vere wrote Shakespeare's plays. For the emerging evidence on Howard's political role, see John Bossy, "After the Rising: Lord Henry Howard and the Earl of Essex: A

parts of the country. These were for bachelors or widowers who "by reasons of age, ill health, accident, or infirmity, shall be unable to maintain themselves by their own exertions."[2] Residents of Shotesham were explicitly included as potential occupants of the largest of these institutions in Greenwich, London. In the late 19th century, a separate alms house was built by the charity overseeing Howard's estate in the village itself. Known as Trinity Hospital, or simply The Greenwich, its eight cottages and central hall are still in use today.

The Somerset House Conference, 1604, by unknown artist. Henry Howard second from right. National Portrait Gallery, London.

Our former home is immediately across the village's main street. Lived in by the Lovewell family for three quarters of a century, the house had origins going back far enough that while we were there we were not quite sure who built it or exactly when. Our best indication was the brief description that resulted from a visit by National Trust representatives during the 1950s: the original house, they said, dated from the 1500s, with a major addition in the 1600s. Their description noted the antique front porch, with ornately carved brackets depicting a lion, a unicorn and satyrs, and a terracotta inscription on a brick gable reading *Veritas odium parit*. I was intrigued by the inscription's meaning—truth begets hatred. It is a line from Lady of Andros by the Roman comic playwright Terence, spoken in the play's opening lines by

....
Reattribution," *Times Literary Supplement*, July 25, 2014, pp. 14–15.
2 Quoted in Geoffrey Gunn, *Shotesham: Brief Account of a Tas Valley Village* (Shotesham: 1976), p. 8.

an Athenian freedman to his former master. There is more to the line than these three words. In full it reads "These days flattery wins friends, truth begets hatred." Of course truth can beget all sorts of things, hatred included. While growing up I liked to think that one of the house's first generations of occupants was telling posterity something about the times they lived in—the fact that the Shotesham of their day was a stratified place, with the lord of the local manor closely controlling life in the village.

Even when I was a boy, the village's main landowning family, named Fellowes, were a force to be reckoned with. Boasting a splendid residence, Shotesham Hall, they inhabited a social stratum well beyond our reach. For example, Robert Fellowes, private secretary to the Queen during the 1990s and husband of Princess Diana's sister Jane Spencer, is from a collateral branch of the family which descends from the first Fellowes who came to Shotesham. We were most familiar with the Reverend Lionel Fellowes. The third Fellowes in a century-long line which had served as vicars of the village parish, he lived in a Georgian rectory, with eighty acres of glebe located next to our farm. A distant figure, he seemed to enjoy his comfortable existence, aided by the services of a chauffeur and full-time gardener, and with the added benefit of having to do very little actual work himself. Not that his good fortune was particularly noteworthy: depositing squires' younger sons in the local benefice was a time-honoured tradition.

Not that all members of the Fellowes family were hidebound in their views. By landowning standards they were relative latecomers to Norfolk. William Fellowes, a lawyer and philanthropist, purchased the estate in the early 18th century. He became known as the Man of Shotesham, reputedly because of his similarity to Alexander Pope's saintly Man of Ross,[3] and showed his forward thinking by opening England's very first cottage hospital in the village and hiring one of the country's best surgeons to staff

....

3   B. K. Blyth, *The Norwich Guide* (Haymarket: 1842), p. 223.

it. His son Robert commissioned architect Sir John Sloan to design a new Shotesham Hall. Just as there were three long-serving Fellowes rectors in the village, so too were there three long-lived Fellowes squires in succession, all named Robert, with William's son being the first. The last of the three, an avid hunter, died at the age of 97 in 1915 and was something of an eccentric even by elastic Victorian standards. During his heyday as lord of the manor it is said he disallowed those of his tenants who attended Shotesham All Saints Church from entering the sanctuary until he had arrived so he could lead them up the aisle, then made sure the village constable was stationed outside afterwards to stop any loitering.[4] By the time of my boyhood these days had long gone, with a far more austere family representative, his grandson Major Charles Fellowes, in charge.

In the 1920s the Fellowes were facing financial difficulties, and with all the changes that began to come fast and furiously in World War I's aftermath it was clear that age-old entitlements such as those enjoyed by Reverend Fellowes were nearing an end. Much else was to undergo radical change in the village in the years after my birth. I was joyously welcomed into the world by my mother at Grove Farm on July 3rd 1929, with the assistance of the village midwife, Nurse Beaden. My early days were cuddled and bathed in the joy of maternal love. I have always known this. Nobody told me. It has been one of the foundation assurances of my life. But I have always had the feeling that my father

---

4 Owen Chadwick, *Victorian Miniature* (Cambridge: 1991), p. 13. Another story about this Robert is related by the noted painter of horses Sir Alfred Munnings, who occasionally visited Shotesham. In his autobiography he recalls, "It was at Shotesham Hall, when I was painting two horses, that I first met the famous Squire Fellowes, then about ninety-two or three. Seeing that the horse I was painting wouldn't prick his ears, he said, 'Go in the house and bring out the footman, who's always playing a Jew's harp.' The man came out and played his Jew's harp, and the horse pricked his ears. At lunch I asked the squire if he knew the name of a certain writer on sport. 'He used to hunt', I said. 'Pshaw! All sorts of monkeys hunt,' said he." *An Artist's Life* (London: 1950), p. 202.

Ernest and his sister Jane, ca. 1917. Lovewell family collection.

was disappointed when the birth of a son was announced. Two years before, when Ivan arrived, he had rejoiced as much as my mother had. My arrival was different. When I listened to family conversations about each of our births, there was a thought that I felt guilty about whenever it flashed into my mind and was entertained with growing resentment—that if my birth had brought forth a girl instead, my father would have abstained for life in order to keep the family with that ideal constituency, a boy and a girl. Beryl would then never have been born. When three years later my uncle Arthur ran into the cowshed to announce the birth of a daughter, my father let out a shout of joy and milked the cow, according to my uncle, faster than he had ever done before or since.

My father, Ernest Lovewell, was born in 1899. That he was only one year in the 19th century could not have been deduced from his attitudes or tastes in life: in no way was he a 20th century man. Living during the previous hundred years would have been less stressful in his struggle to survive as a Christian, a farmer and a father. For him the rapid changes during his own lifespan were bewildering. He needed time to experience and absorb anything new, and his slowness of response caused him to stop trying to keep up. By his fifties he had retreated into a world of his own. It is significant that at about this time he became hard of hearing. He was thereby able to shut out the voices of the doomed world and the unfaithful church. He never learned to drive a tractor or a car and was left to enjoy the horses which he kept on the farm until he retired.

The church had always been the centre of his life, but when that institution changed along with the rest of the world the Bible became his final refuge and prayer his principal conversation. One climactic day he announced that we would no longer be taking the News Chronicle, a national newspaper, because all that we needed to know about the world, past, present, and future, could be found in the Bible, especially the books of the Old Testament prophets, whose effect extended even to his geopolitical views, with his strong sense that those nations which supported the Jews would receive God's favour. The Norwich paper, the Eastern Daily Press, escaped the fate of the News Chronicle, either because my mother dug in her heels or because it specialized in local news, so devoted only a small space to the world that had run amok. He rarely picked it up, but others could. The great intruder was the radio, but on Sundays that did at least bring a service into the kitchen.

My mother, Gladys Black, was born in 1901. That one year into the 20th century made all the difference. Able to cope with change and with ears and eyes wide open, she had a quick mind and a keen memory. The church was the centre of her life too. She met Father because her own father was a local preacher in the Methodist circuit of which Shotesham was a part.

Once my parents settled down together, Mother was constantly frustrated by Father's slowness and accommodated it by making him her boy for whom she did just about everything. As he was unable to match anything up, each morning she would lay out the clothes he was to wear. His collar studs were forever being misplaced and he invariably called to her to find them for him. "Mother," he would bawl out from upstairs, "where's my tie? Mother, where's my collar? Mother, which socks did you want me to wear?" She did as bidden, her needs satisfied as much as his.

David E. Lovewell

It was an unlikely match, but for my mother a desirable one. The Blacks were poor, with few financial prospects, but the Lovewells were farmers, landed people. Not that it was loveless; in the early years it seems to have had its share of romance. Letters, now sadly lost, which Ivan, Beryl and I once came across to our delight in a drawer in their bedroom, indicate a lively courtship. But at some point stoic Christian commitment took over, keeping them together until death. Yes, there was a continuing love, but mixed with impatience, resentment and obedience to God. The negative feelings were dealt with either by burying them or by silent prayer and confession. They were never admitted to the family.

In pragmatic terms, the two of them were good for one another. Father knew how to farm, grow crops, tend cattle, milk cows: he was an exceedingly capable farmer, and in recognition of that fact we would often give tours of our farm to visitors from the Norfolk chapter of the National Farmers Union. Mother knew how to do the rest. Like her own lay preacher father she was ambitious, resolute, gregarious, voluble, a presence to be reckoned with. It was a bit of a joke at first that Father had married someone untutored in village ways, let alone farming. After the wedding and her move into the large farmhouse, there are stories of the city girl trying hard to speedily become a good farmer's wife. But her new neighbours soon discovered she was no slouch in adapting herself to this new environment.

It was she who kept the books, and watched over the business side of the family's livelihood. Whereas she was volatile, a Black trait, Father was calm. She was calculating, he naïve. They met each other's demands for emotional balance and for earning a prosperous living. There was a deep concern for people rooted in both of them. Father's concern was based on the Bible. Whenever anyone asked him for anything he gave it without question: "Give to him who begs from you, and do not refuse him who would borrow from you." His generosity became a frustration for me and Ivan as we got old enough to see him taken in by scroungers.

He was easily duped and deeply hurt when he realized that some people didn't live up to their words. In his eyes, "I'll pay you back soon," was a promise that would surely be kept.

Mother's concern for people was more a natural response. She learned it in the poverty of her childhood. She entered into the life of the village's Methodist chapel with great enthusiasm. She also developed a little parish of needy people for whom she felt pastorally responsible. The local medic, Dr. Gibson, would often call on her to assist in his care for the village sick and asked that she be present with him at births he suspected would be difficult. She could have had a rewarding career in any number of professional pursuits, but the stultifying class system of her early days prevented anything of that sort. For such a dream that she must have entertained she was born to the wrong people—not for character, but simply for the money. Instead she married: rescuing Father, protecting him in his vulnerability. Any other kind of marriage would have been his destruction. Or perhaps his making?

The author and Ivan, probably in 1932. Lovewell family collection.

Mother, too, had someone she leaned on. Lily Pegg was a village girl who needed a job. Grabbing at the opportunity, she entered service at our house when she was fourteen and became part of the family for six days a week. Housework, child care and acting as dairy maid filled her life for twelve hours a day for almost thirty years. I have fond memories of her leading me on walks, bathing me, and taking me to her home on Friday afternoons after her mother, Mrs. Pegg, had finished baking bread. I soon developed a penchant for those freshly made loaves, lashed with farm butter: crusty, warm, delicious. After a few visits Mrs. Pegg made a small round loaf especially for me, baked in a fruit can cut off about halfway so that the small loaf would rise to a cauliflower shape, waiting to be sliced in half, buttered, and eaten. I would consume half of it there and take the rest home for my tea to be slowly consumed before a jealous Ivan. Only a few things could make him jealous. I was jealous of him most of the time. "The Boy," as he was known within the family, seemed to get all the attention, the kind of attention his younger brother "Boy David" longed for.

Much of this was predictable in a family such as ours. Ivan was first son in a farmer's household where primogeniture was automatically assumed. Some of it related to our respective characters as well. Although he and I spent much time together, his interests tended to be ones that he worked on alone. Never idle, he was able to concentrate at a task for many hours. A gift for sketching surfaced early, and later in life he became an accomplished artist. He also enjoyed making things. One of his earliest hobbies was creating model aircraft and ships. He acquired a fretsaw and crafted numerous plaques and gadgets out of plywood. He also liked gardening and, when he was about six or seven, had a plot set aside for him where he specialized in lettuce, radish, carrots and red beet. Once he reached twelve he started tending the greenhouse and grew tomatoes and grapes. And at about this time he also took up photography.

At school Ivan shone at field sports, especially running. But as he entered his teens his attention focused more and more on the farm. At fifteen, he dropped out of school and began working for Father full time. His impact upon farm affairs was immediately visible not just to those of us who worked with him but to anyone who happened to pass by our fields. An agricultural art that the county of Norfolk was famous for was the roofing and thatching of haystacks to protect them from the weather. This requires positioning rows of sheaves in a roofing pattern, then placing carefully cut thatch on top of this row. It was a task tailor-made for someone with Ivan's talents. As a young teenager he developed the knack for creating large and beautifully shaped stacks that could be seen and admired from long distances.

Eventually he purchased and took over the three farms, Grove Farm, Hill Farm and Valley Farm, that Father had brought together. His attachment to the land fascinated me. When he was in his sixties I recall suggesting to him that he should sell the farm and enjoy a life of leisure, pursuing his many interests. His response was that the farm didn't belong to him, he belonged to the farm. When he finally did retire and departed the farm in his seventies, it was due to deteriorating health.

One of Ivan's crowning achievements was receiving two awards from the Queen for his active concern for the environment. He found that in some areas on the farm there were rare species of plants, and he set those areas aside for special protection. His knowledge of the local flora was exceptional. To walk with Ivan over the farm was to learn about plants and their uses as well as the folklore attached to them. And while he learned the craft of farming from a successful farmer, Ivan took the practical aspects of farming to an entirely new level. He ran what can only be described as a model farm: pristine, meticulously well-ordered, up to date, highly efficient.

Beryl was five years younger than Ivan and three years younger than me—enough of a gap that it was noticeable to all three of us while growing up. My relationship with Beryl was always an easy one, and when she reached her teens, especially her late teens, we became and remained close friends. She made her mark very early, thanks to natural ebullience that shone through in her character as well as a rapidly developed talent for music, which appeared when she was just three or four. Very soon she took on a key part in holiday gatherings, as she encouraged us to gather about the family's piano so we could sing along with her playing.

Our repertoire included popular songs and, of course, Methodist hymns.

Very soon Beryl was regularly playing the organ at chapel as well. It was a remarkable sight to see someone so young perform in public with utter confidence. Ivan and I both dabbled in music, but, uncharacteristically for Ivan, he never pursued this hobby beyond playing a few scales. My own attempts to master guitar playing came later and did not amount to much either.

But right from the start I had the gift of the gab. I was born to talk and talk I did, taking advantage whenever I could find a willing audience. It was therefore inevitable that I would find my way to the chapel pulpit, something I did by the age of fourteen. Grandpa Black's career as a local preacher helped. I would often accompany him to his preaching appointments throughout the Methodist circuit. Sensing my interest, he soon had me reading the scriptures and eventually gave me the opportunity to take a brief part in the sermons. And so, just as Ivan was the artist, craftsman and farming enthusiast and Beryl the musician, I too carved out a distinctive role in family life thanks to my quick tongue and taste for showmanship.

Perhaps it was this love of the limelight that caused me to throw a bit of a spanner—or more literally, a finger—into the works when I was just three. It was the day after Beryl was born. Ivan and I were playing in the barn with what should have been a harmless hand-cranked cake crusher, a machine that broke slabs of linseed into bite-sized niblets for cows. Ivan idly turned the handle as I inspected the insides where the hidden work of crushing was accomplished. The scream that suddenly followed was even louder than the din of the tractor and the oat-grinding mill together. Uncle Arthur was nearby. He was Mother's youngest brother, at that point in his early teens: a bit of a troubled soul who was living with us and was of special concern for Mother, so that she had taken on a maternal role.

A Place in the Sun

He heard my cry straight away and grabbed that bloodied, frightened three year old lying on the floor at the foot of the cake crusher. Bundled in his arms I was carried across the yard towards the house, followed by a bewildered Ivan. I was taken straight to the farm kitchen. Lily was there, while Mother was upstairs in bed with Beryl. Mother heard the screams and knew it was me. She also knew it was out of the ordinary. "What's the matter with David?" she called out. "Oh nothing, he fell down and cut himself; you know David, can't stay on his feet for long," said Lily. Mother could not be fooled. "It's more than that."

A neighbouring farmer, Mr. Shannahan, had a car. There were a few other car owners in the village, but they couldn't be called on, even in such an emergency. Major Fellowes, and his brother Reverend Fellowes, were somewhat out of reach by village class distinctions, as was Mr. Barton, a well-off financier who worked in Norwich and lived in the big house opposite the village school. These people were not available—it wouldn't have felt right to ask them. But Mr. Shannahan was a farmer, and Uncle Arthur knew he would help out. "Of course I'll drive the young bugger to hospital," Mr. Shannahan said when asked. Nurse Beaden was called and soon arrived. She wrapped my left hand in bandages that soon became a big red ball at the end of my arm. I sat on her knee in the front of Mr. Shannahan's car and was driven to the Norfolk and Norwich Hospital.

The inside of the hospital was white: white walls, white ceilings, white sinks, white floors, white tables, and white aproned nurses. One of them took me from Nurse Beaden, who was always dressed in navy blue. I was taken through a white door. At this point my memory, or my imagination, fades.

Uncle Arthur, some years after, when we were cycling past the hospital, drew my attention to smoke coming out of the tall hospital chimney stack. "Is it a finger or a toe they're burning today?" I knew exactly what he meant. It answered forever the question that had puzzled me about the top of my badly crushed finger that had been cut off by my doctor.

"Any distinguishing marks?" the passport enquires. "Half of third finger on left hand amputated." That stubby finger retains its pointed message for me. It is a constant reminder of my jealous nature that so often threatens my most intimate relationships. Somehow, buried deep in my psyche, it has become associated with the brief attention I stole from my sister Beryl the day after she displaced me. Was I jealous of her presence in my home? I had been the centre of attention for three years from Mother and from Lily. But now a baby sister innocently shattered all that. Today when I become jealous, fearing the loss of some crucial relationship, dreading to be left alone, forced to fantasize the sudden absence of a person on whom my existence seems to depend, I look at my "distinguishing mark" and try to recover my equilibrium before I strike out with words I might later regret.

Chapter 2: Early School Days

Every day in term the bell of the village school was rung by the headmistress Mrs. Howse a few minutes before the hour at 9 and again at 1, its peals audible throughout much of Shotesham. The tiny school house, in a converted cottage that dated back to Tudor times, contained two classrooms, one for beginners taught by Mrs. Danes, the other for everybody else. This latter room was partitioned by a curtain. In one of these makeshift spaces Miss Thorpe oversaw the middle forms, while just beyond the curtain the eldest students were taught by Mrs. Howse. Of these three, Mrs. Danes was the friendliest. Mrs. Howse and Miss Thorpe were disciplinarians, grudgingly respected, but not much loved.

In September 1934, on my very first school day, Ivan escorted me on the walk from our house. Up until then virtually all of my time was spent on the farm, and whenever I did leave its Eden-like precincts it was in the company of adults. This time walking the distance of the village's long winding street and past The Greenwich to the schoolhouse next to Church Hill was a major adventure, though my excitement was mixed with fear as we approached the alien new world. I remember seeing the school's cloak room for the first time. At its dark green sinks, with jugs of water standing underneath, we were expected to wash our hands before entering class. The towels hanging on rollers gave off a pungent smell of soap and dirt. A disagreeable odour, but one I would become accustomed to.

When we entered my classroom Mrs. Danes was already there. She smiled at Ivan. "So this is your brother who you've told me all about." She turned to me. "You're going to like it here," she said. And I did. Once Ivan left for Miss Thorpe's class, I opened

David E. Lovewell

View from Church Hill. Courtesy Ken Brockway and The Walking Englishman website at www.walkingenglishman.com

the desk which Mrs. Danes pointed out for me to sit at. Inside was a slate and stylus. Missing were paper, pen and ink, which would come later. But there was a table heaped with books at the side of the room and next to it an open toy box. As I surveyed my new surroundings, the room slowly filled up. Some faces I knew, but I was taken aback by the realization that there were children in our village I'd never seen before. Several weeks would have to pass for us to overcome our shyness with one another.

In those same few weeks we also settled into our regimented day, which Mrs. Danes did her best to enliven. Most memorable was inspection time. Every morning after prayers she would ask us to step away from our desks so we could stand in a long single line and hold out our hands. Stopping in front of each of us, she took hold of the ends of our fingers to check that our nails were clean. One of our classmates, Jimmy Goodrum, virtually always had dirty fingernails. That meant he was regularly required to go to the sinks to wash them. He told me afterwards that it was fun to do so while the rest of us got down to our lessons. He would often be absent for a long time, sometimes so long that Mrs. Danes had to dart out of the classroom to retrieve him from the cloak room.

Jimmy's clothes were in the same state as his fingernails. I mentioned this once to Mother, who replied that I should be thankful to have a well-tended home to come back to. I also needed to be thankful that our house was plentifully stocked with handkerchiefs. For besides providing our outstretched hands for inspection we also had to show Mrs. Danes that we always had a hanky with us. One day, when it came to inspection time, I discovered I'd forgotten mine. How this happened was a mystery, as Mother's last comment each day before I left the house was a reminder to check that I had one.

Mrs. Danes was coming down the line, nearer and nearer. Luckily I was standing next to Jimmy. Seeing my plight he pulled out a second hanky—blue with white polka dots. I'd never seen one like it before: ours were all Methodist white. Mrs. Danes didn't notice Jimmy hand it to me. He was good at doing things without being seen. And it worked, though Mrs. Danes, after glancing at the hanky, looked at me and then at Jimmy, but said nothing. Jimmy was my friend from that day on—dirt or no dirt.

The schoolhouse had a large fireplace. On cold days it held a blaze that warmed our room as well as water pipes that passed through the wall to the room occupied by the older children. When the fire's heat was particularly intense, we could hear unsettling bubbling sounds in the pipes. One day we were busy at our lessons when this sound was followed by a sudden bout of splashing as boiling water spurted from the rimmed joint between the pipe and a small tank high on the wall. The bubbling deluge rapidly filled the room with steam. All of us, including Mrs. Danes, erupted in screams. Opening the door to the other classroom, she had no need to say a thing. We ran, pushing and shoving each other through the doorway, and somehow all got through, with Mrs. Danes the last out of the room. Miss Thorpe, in the curtained section of the room next to us, was startled by the sudden invasion. Ivan was at his desk. I glanced over and our eyes met. My fright was soon replaced by secret pleasure. I would have a story to tell at that night's tea table. But in spite of all the evening's brave talk, from then on I was suspicious of that patch of pipe high in the wall. Many times I looked up and wondered if it held any more surprises. I longed to move up into next year's class with Ivan, even if it meant enduring Miss Thorpe's harshness.

The next year, she turned out to be as strict as schoolyard gossips had advertised. Unlike Mrs. Danes, she had little hesitation in reporting troublemakers to Mrs. Howse, and that usually meant getting the cane in front of both Miss Thorpe's and Mrs. Howse's classes. My own attention-getting ways did not extend to a penchant for public punishment, but some of my classmates were made of sterner stuff. One boy in particular impressed us all. His name was Sydney Sexton (his father was a talented amateur artist whose paintings of the village I still own today). After a caning he kept out his hand and with a calm smirk said, "Do it again, it tickles." As his reputation with the rest of us vaulted upwards, Mrs. Howse's mouth dropped. No words came out. Her only recourse was a note sent home with Sydney for his parents. To all appearances this too failed to bother Sydney. He told us later that he would never in a million years give that note to his father. I'm sure I wasn't the only one, however, who realized that he hadn't mentioned whether his mother was included in that statement.

When viewed from the distance of time, such displays of Mrs. Howse's discipline were fairly mild—certainly when compared with the punishments which, according to legend, had once reigned at the school. In the decades after the schoolhouse had first opened in the 1870s, it was said of the headmistress, a certain Miss Best, that she had a special nuttery-stick full of knots as her

A Place in the Sun

Shotesham students in about 1935, with the author on the rocking horse. Courtesy Daphne Smith and Heather Jackson

method for ensuring good conduct. If a miscreant proved especially intransigent, Miss Best brought in outside aid in the form of the village rector, a Reverend Fellowes from before our time, who would deal with the perpetrator with his hunting crop.

So we could hardly complain about Mrs. Howse's cane. On the whole, my two years in Miss Thorpe's class were uneventful. Most memorably the academic demands on us were delightfully light. With no thought at the village school of giving students homework, Ivan, I and our classmates were left with abundant time for more important things—climbing haystacks, puttering about at the Beck, and concocting complicated games of hide and seek in the various meadows and copses on the farm. The fact that the school was so close to home was a boon. So too was our proximity to the village's main grocery store, owned by Mr. Laws, which stood opposite the schoolhouse. The Shop, as we called it, was small but managed to carry just about everything: flour, bacon, beans, paraffin, cotton, buttons, wool, cigarettes, oranges and sweets. Before Guy Fawkes Night every November, Mr. Laws would stock fireworks as well. With the arrival of autumn we would join the Shop's fireworks club, taking a few pennies each week and having Mr. Laws mark down our accumulating funds. For the rest of the year it was candy that gave meaning to our weekly allowance—and the reason we usually referred to it as "sweet money."

After lunch each Tuesday, Ivan and I were given a penny each by Mother. We then returned to school earlier than usual so that we could visit the Shop. Pushing open the door and listening for the bell to ring in Mr. Laws' front room, right next to the store, we would look up at the large glass jars on the shelves behind the cluttered counter and view the possible delights for the afternoon: licorice sticks to chew slowly at playtime, sherbet to suck through a straw from a coloured bag, toffees, chocolates, smarties, hearts, gob-stoppers, chewing gum. My new school friends like Jimmy were a problem on sweet day; some would even come and help to select, and I knew what that meant.

In the meantime Mother was growing increasingly disenchanted with the village school. In her view it wouldn't prepare us adequately for what she envisioned for each of our futures. For Father it was different. Since, in his mind, Ivan and I were to be farmers, the most important part of our education would be working with him, and an apprenticeship was far more useful than anything learned from a book. We would have to do our lessons, of course, because there was much we needed to learn, but there was a limit.

As usual, it was Mother's opinion that carried the day, and it was one of the lay preachers of our acquaintance who helped her hatch a plan. When preachers and ministers visited our chapel on a Sunday, it was customary for them to take a service at 3 in the afternoon, then another at 6:30. Most would come to our home for tea to pass the time between. Mr. Gibbs was a teacher at Bracondale, a school on the south edge of Norwich, just six

A Place in the Sun

and a half miles from Shotesham. He and Mother talked a good deal about our education, with Mr. Gibbs stressing the constraints that staying at Shotesham school could impose on both of us. In the 1930s, council schools such as ours struggled with various challenges: multiple classes taught in a single room, students from a wide range of backgrounds, and many parents who had little interest in the academic progress of their offspring. Looking back, I realize why it might be that both Miss Thorpe and Mrs. Howse felt they needed to be as strict as they were. In such a setting, few students tended to pursue further education. Success depended on passing a scholarship exam at eleven. If the scholarship was won, the student would be able to go to a grammar school free of charge. It was a most coveted award. But the grammar school was Anglican, hence anathema to us. Mr. Gibbs suggested that Ivan and I switch to Bracondale instead. It would mean paying a fee, but we would have the benefit of a guaranteed high school education otherwise impossible for Methodists. This convinced Mother, and what convinced her was fine with Father. And in retrospect, she was absolutely right: in the circumstances Bracondale was the perfect choice for both her sons. It was relatively old by Norwich standards, dating back to the 1820s, when its founder, a certain D. B. Hickey, launched it "to produce happy and decent young gentlemen who do their best, and have consideration for the welfare and feelings of others." True to this stated purpose, the school's emphasis was more on character-building than on academic accomplishment, a mandate that appealed to the city burghers and prosperous farmers from the nearby countryside who sent their sons there.

There was one slight problem. Bracondale was a boys' school and most of the teachers were men, while at Shotesham we had grown used to having women teachers. Mother felt it would be necessary to ease us gently into such a setting. To accomplish this, we were to be sent for a year to the neighbouring village of Poringland. Its school had two men as teachers and a reputation for effective discipline—just the place to toughen us up for Bracondale's male-dominated environment.

So, starting in September 1937, Ivan and I had a daily commute by bike to Poringland. The village boys took offense at our departure. "Stuck up," they called us, and they made noises that they would no longer be our friends. This took getting used to, and we faced the prospect of dealing with a new set of classmates. As it happened, our aunt and uncle, Mother's brother Cyril and his wife Olive, lived just a few hundred yards from our new school. It was arranged that we have lunches there. Thus we had some element of familiarity.

There were twice as many students at Poringland as at Shotesham, and on our first morning Ivan and I found the classrooms crowded. I was despondent when I discovered I would again be separated from Ivan, but relieved by the sight of my teacher. Mr. Brown was a big, jolly man who proved to be extremely knowledgeable. For him, every question had an answer, even questions that had nothing to do with our lesson, or even with school. Before the start of each school day there would be a group around his desk, talking with him, asking him questions, showing him something to do with our hobbies. He was always interested. From that first day I found myself listening to his soft voice, comforted by the sight of eyes that weren't looking for something that was wrong. School was exciting once more, as it had been in my very first year with Mrs. Danes, though this was a different kind of excitement.

Our aunt and uncle's home was beside a large wood. After lunch there was time for Ivan and me to explore this new territory of chestnut, walnut, oak, elm, ash, pine and fir. Some of these trees were made for clambering; others defied ascent because of their high branches. We were continually warned not to climb with our school clothes on, but the wood's attractions were so tempting that such warnings went unheeded. Of all the trees there, the chestnuts were our favourite, as they provided the material for a

A Place in the Sun

Some of Poringland School's class of 1937. Courtesy the Poringland Archive at www.poringlandarchive.co.uk/poringland

popular schoolyard game known as conkers. A small meat skewer, or, if one was fortunate enough, a pocket knife with a skewer-like blade attached, was needed to bore a hole through the centre of the chestnut. A string was then threaded through the bored hole, a knot tied at one end, and about fifteen inches was kept loose to ensure a good strong swing. The purpose of the game was to smash an opponent's conker. The victories associated with a particular conker were added together and boasted about. A tenner, twentier, or even a hundreder were theoretically possible, and because nobody could check on the actual number of victories, reputed hundreders were a very common species.

Another playground excitement was a fight. Some were sparked over genuine differences or a seething sense of injustice, but many were meant only to draw a crowd. I started one with a boy whose name I cannot recall, and after a few punches the crowd gathered. My name was being shouted by some, but the other boy's name seemed to be shouted much more loudly. That in itself took the wind out of me. As soon as we began exchanging blows I knew

I was done for. With an eye-watering jab of his clenched fist, my opponent showed he was no stranger to schoolyard brawls. I put all I had into my punches but got knocked flat, my nose bleeding. An awful cheer went up and I was left on the ground as the crowd melted away. Soon only Ivan was standing next to me. He asked what the fight had been about. I didn't want to say that I'd started it and really didn't know why. Then and there, in my embarrassment, I resolved that it wasn't worth starting a fight unless there was something to fight over. I would just have to find other ways of getting attention.

The year at Poringland passed quickly, the summer of 1938 arriving with the freedom of the farmyard, fields and fresh air awaiting us. All of this was then capped off with the thrill of harvest. Father allowed Ivan and me the opportunity to continue our boyish amusements. Soon enough we would be part of the close-at-hand labour pool which most farmers felt obliged to draw on. The only uncertainty that loomed was our upcoming move to be day boys at Bracondale. One glorious summer's day we were pulled away from our play for a visit to the school so it could be decided which classes we would be enrolled in. While our parents spoke with the junior school's headmaster Mr. Wheeler, Ivan and I loitered on the school's front lawn to watch a bi-plane towing a glider through the sky. It was an appropriate sight. We were ushered inside a small study room used by the school's boarders. Mr. Wheeler gave Ivan some sums to work on and me a book to read out loud. I was relieved when I learned I would be placed in the class of boys my own age.

When school began that September, Mother took us by car. Again the thought of being by myself left me despondent. Ironically, given all of the planning around male teachers that had gone into this move, my homeroom teacher that year was a woman. When I entered my new class Mrs. Hardy was at her seat in the centre of an open 'U' formation of desks. As Mrs. Danes had done years before, she made a point of speaking to me before the class began. "David Lovewell?" "Yes." "That's a nice name. You have a brother at school with you don't you?" "Yes." "You live on a farm?" "Yes." "Do you have any animals on your farm?" "Yes." "You will have a chance later to tell us about the farm." And just as before I knew I would like her.

After we had sung a hymn and Mrs. Hardy had read a story from the Bible, we were each given a turn to speak about anything we wanted to share: holidays, harvest, the seaside, our farm. This was when I realized that not only Mrs. Hardy, but the rest of the class, listened to me. All were quiet as I spoke. Over the weeks, I told them about how old our house was. I added a hundred years just to make sure they kept listening. Then I told them how I lost my finger—some had already asked and I'd related the story to them, but it was worth telling everyone. I told them how much pain I still got from it in the winter time. That was only a little bit true, and when I sat down I felt badly, not just about adding a century to the house's age but also the number of rooms and the kinds of things that were in them. I knew I shouldn't exaggerate, but who would know the difference?

Bracondale brought other benefits as well. Often on Thursday afternoons we had an outing to some attraction in the city: the Cathedral, the Castle Museum, Black Friar's Hall, Caley's chocolate factory, the YWCA's underground swimming pool at a converted stately home known as Samson and Hercules House. On at least one other afternoon each week, Mr. Wheeler—Cherry to all of us because of the colour of his face—read aloud from *Wind in the Willows*, *Gulliver's Travels*, *Travels with a Donkey in the Cévennes*, and *Treasure Island*, books which still hold a special place in my imagination today.

Each midday our classroom became a dining room, and we were served a hot meal by the school's matron. Heaping plates of bread, sliced from long square loaves with leathery crusts, were followed by a hot course. My favourite was minced beef. It was accompanied by potatoes and vegetables from the school gardens, a small slice of crispy toast planted on top. Then came dessert—stewed fruit or some other kind of pudding, always laced with Bird's custard—finished with a mug of tea. There was only one thing wrong with these meals: there was never enough. After lunch when we were allowed to go out of the school grounds for a walk we would make for the fish and chip shop just around the corner. Ivan and I had more than a penny a week in allowance now, and we spent it all on chips. Later once we had advanced to Bracondale's senior school we would order fish as well—we had more pocket money then.

That first year at Bracondale passed and break-up day for the summer holidays came slowly, so very slowly. But then we had eight carefree weeks at home on the farm. Our village friends had only five weeks. They continued to taunt us about abandoning them, and about our uniforms and all the other paraphernalia our parents had had to buy for us when we had started at the school. Not least they resented the new friends we were bringing home. For them, we were trying to be 'la-tee-da', and they could still beat us in a fight any day we wanted one. I can't recall there ever being a fight, and thankfully they gradually stopped their teasing and threats and we got on good terms again. That restoration of friendship made me happy that summer of 1939—the last gasp of childhood before the changes that lay just around the corner.

I am not sure whether it is just my memory playing tricks, but that last summer of peacetime seemed to bring particularly glorious weather and an especially abundant harvest. But as the weeks went by it became ever harder, even for boys like us, to ignore all that was happening in the wider world.

We had already had some exposure to what might loosely be termed a wartime mindset. Our gym teacher that first year at Bracondale was a man named Sergeant Row. A former gymnast and professional soldier, he was determined to make us fit to be British Tommies in the event that war did happen and lasted long enough for youngsters such as us to be recruited. We learned to march in all kinds of weather with flags and complicated-looking displays of what appeared to be martial precision, though the maneuvers were in fact quite simple. He shouted his orders in good sergeant-major style and it was not unknown for him to clip a boy's ears with the back of his hand. We dutifully obeyed as we were ridiculed into shape for one hour two days a week. All we lacked as a school boy army were proper uniforms and guns.

On sports day that year our parents turned out to see our drills. For them, Sergeant Row was a godsend. "He teaches discipline... He doesn't put up with any rudeness...A pity the older boys didn't have this kind of training...They wouldn't be half so lazy or saucy." Our views on his character were a little less positive. He had no mercy, and we couldn't help but note that he didn't go to church or chapel. While two of our teachers, Mr. Robinson-Glasgow and Miss Southgate, became involved with one another and would later get engaged, we boys could never imagine Sergeant having a wife. He wasn't a woman's man at all. A friend I made at Bracondale, Wally Hemmant, once said, "Do you think Sergeant has ever kissed a woman?" (Actually he didn't use the word kiss.) I could imagine Sergeant shooting somebody, even a woman, but not kissing them. As for Mr. Robinson-Glasgow and Miss Southgate, they spent a lot of time together before their engagement. There was no difficulty to imagine them kissing. They left after they got engaged and I never saw them again. The Sergeant, on the other hand, stayed on to inflict more pain on us.

David E. Lovewell

Chapter 3: The War Years

One morning in September 1938 Mother was baking bread in the kitchen. My aunt Violet, her sister, was visiting and they were talking of the Munich Crisis. "When this is over," I overheard Violet say, "there is bound to be another crisis and then there will be war." The matter-of-factness of her words struck me. I remember walking out to the back lawn in a daze, not sure whether to be alarmed or thrilled. I pictured trenches and fighting, British Tommies shooting and bayoneting hundreds of Germans. I was there with them, bayonet in hand, hacking away at the enemy. Joe, the dog, leashed nearby, was with me in the thick of the fray, excited by my shouting and dashing about.

Violet strode out of the kitchen, obviously at Mother's behest. "Stop teasing Joe." But I wasn't teasing him. Joe knew perfectly well what was happening, and was primed to help in any way he could. He had recently bitten a salesman on his ankle and the salesman had come to the front door to make a fuss. Father had said then that he wished Joe would bite a few more salesmen so they wouldn't keep coming around and interrupting his work. Joe would do his bit in the war. If the Germans invaded he would be a good companion. I often watched him chewing bones from Sunday's roast. They cracked and crunched and broke into pieces. No wonder the salesman gave a shout when Joe nipped his ankle.

I had no idea whether Aunt Violet's statement that morning would come true, but it piqued my curiosity. Father had not enlisted when he had come of age near the end of World War I, but his elder brothers, my uncles Alfred and George, had been infantrymen. Another of my uncles on Father's side, Bernard, has been a tank corps captain, and was among the first to drive a tank into battle in France. At family gatherings, Alfred and George sometimes told stories, always funny, but never talked about fighting. I remember Alfred saying "It was me who won the war. The rest stood and watched." When I asked George if he'd killed anyone, he just nodded. "Bullet or bayonet?" I continued. "You don't really want to know," he replied. As for Bernard, I never heard him mention his fighting days at all.

In the final months of 1938 and then during the first part of 1939, war talk in the village intensified, though I now realize that my parents, like so many, were doing their best to keep this talk from Ivan, Beryl and me. The day that war was declared, September 3rd, was a Sunday. It dawned like any other with bacon and eggs at our breakfast table, but when it was announced that Neville Chamberlain would address the nation at 11 AM we knew what his speech meant. His famed words that morning cast a chill: "As of this hour we exist in a state of war with Germany." Despite the lead-up of the previous months, my parents were heavily affected by the news. That day, after church, they took turns leading us in prayer around the tea table. Father was always very serious when he prayed, and he would search for his words slowly. I was always reminded of Elijah, one of his favourite Old Testament prophets, when I witnessed him at these moments. There was kindness in his voice, but he also had a sternness, as I imagined Elijah possessed as well. As usual, he spoke of righteousness and justice. When it was Mother's turn she mentioned our names that we might be protected whatever would happen in the months and years ahead. Her voice softened when she prayed. She prayed for people.

From that moment, I never doubted that we would all come through. Because Mother had confidently predicted it and prayed for it, God would comply, and now that our fate was in his hands there was no more doubt. Father, too, confidently predicted victory. Righteousness and mercy were not on Hitler's side. God would never allow the Germans to win, and terrible would be God's judgment on them. But after all the fighting was done they would be forgiven.

The months that followed had an air of unreality about them. We entered that period of limbo before the start of the Battle of France in the spring of 1940 which came to be called the Phoney War. Because of our proximity to the coast, we were in a part of the country that might speedily feel the effects of any ground invasion. Already that summer, soldiers had been working at Poringland, building eight huge pylons, each about three hundred feet high. There were rumours that anti-aircraft guns were hidden behind the hedges and fences surrounding the pylons. Some said the pylons were a secret weapon that Britain had invented to stop the engines of a plane without firing a shot. Others said that they would be able to explode a bomb just as it was ejected, thereby blowing up the plane. We would learn later that the pylons were in fact part of the radar network that covered the eastern and southern coasts of England. One more visible change to the countryside occurred almost immediately: all road signposts were removed, as if invading German troops would not be furnished with accurate maps.

In Norwich, the streets were plastered with colorful propaganda posters—"Freedom is in peril, defend it with all your might." "Your courage, your cheerfulness and your resolution will bring us victory." "Be like Dad, keep Mum." And for our relatives in the city there was now rationing to contend with. We too were under rations, but being on a farm we were able to make do with home-grown vegetables, the produce of our orchards and hedgerows, and local game: rabbits, pheasant, and other sorts of wild meat and fowl we were already well used to.

Like everyone else, we learned to cover windows, inspectors ensuring that not the narrowest slit showed through. For some villagers this meant thick blackout curtains. We had fitted plywood shutters, attached outside on the downstairs windows and inside upstairs, to keep in the light and as potential protection from flying glass. Our car's headlights were fitted with specially designed dimmers which shone down onto the road rather than straight ahead. When driving in fog, or on a dark night, one of us in the car would have to get out and walk in front to lead the way.

At Bracondale air raid shelters were dug under the lawns at the front of the junior school. They were deep narrow trenches, shored up and headed with strong looking oak beams and covered with soil sown with grass to make the shelters look part of the lawn. We were told to bring a tin containing iron rations: items like Horlicks tablets, dry biscuits and chocolate bars to keep us going if we were trapped for several days. We each had a particular place in the shelter, and these rations were stored above our section. It so happened that we never needed them, though at times we spent two or three hours during air raid warnings. We did a lot of talking in the darkness during the time we spent there, and I can remember telling a serial story of a never-ending journey that I made up as I went along. It felt good to have four or five boys listening, and asking me to continue the next time we went down.

Bracondale adjoined the property of Coleman's mustard factory, and immediately adjacent to the playground was a tall plane-spotting tower that was part of the air raid warning system for Norwich. When enemy planes were seen coming over the coast, twenty miles away, the sirens would sound. As soon as they wailed, sometimes two or three times a day, we would pick up our gas masks and dash for the shelters. Concerned about the effect on our education, Bracondale's administrators linked the school to the crash warning system used by Coleman's which went off only when enemy planes were just outside the city. After this we spent much less time down the shelters, but when the warning bells went off we ran helter-skelter below. Not much happened in the way of actual air raids until late in that first school year during the war, but we got practice for when the real thing came.

David E. Lovewell

Farmers like us were expected to cultivate every inch of arable land. In our case, this had an interesting result. Directly next to Grove Farm was a nudist colony taking up seventy acres. Ever since the nudists had begun renting it, its fields had been allowed to grow over. Much to the delight of Ivan and myself, Father was ordered by Ministry officials to clear and cultivate the land. Ivan and I, as well as Ivan's friend Tommy Nicholson, used a tractor with a winch to remove all the trees and bushes to make way for planting. The colonists tended to be upper crust residents of Norwich seeking a few days of fresh air and relaxation. Having never seen nude adults before—certainly not our parents in that state—this was a revelation of the most secular kind.

In May the radio buzzed with the name of an obscure French coastal town. The British army had been rescued and many small boats from fishing villages along England's southeast coast had taken part. Bits of the story filtered into the village from relatives and travelers, but it was Churchill who announced what a victory Dunkirk had been, given so many soldiers successfully evacuated. He told us that it was the ordinary people in small boats who had enabled this, and that they had showed it would take all of us to eventually win the war. It was around that time that the call went out to men to join the Local Defense Volunteers, soon renamed the Home Guard. The village recruits were soon practicing with noisy dummy ammunition and firecrackers serving as grenades. On one occasion I remember Ivan, me and our village friends watching from Church Hill as the volunteers defended the village in a war game against an invading battalion.

I began taking a deep interest in the momentous events taking place around us. Any day I wasn't at school I would eagerly listen to the BBC news at 1 in the afternoon and then at 6 after tea with Father. Mr. Robinson-Glasgow was my teacher that first school year of the war. He told us to cut out the maps from the newspapers and make a war atlas to follow the course of events. "It will help in your geography," he said. I did this, and he was right. But

I had a sinking feeling as the map of German occupation grew larger and talk of invasion became part of everyday conversation.

In the summer of 1940, with the Battle of Britain waging overhead, our farm hands in the Home Guard were issued Lee-Enfield rifles and bayonets. The men still had very little ammunition, but at least they looked like soldiers. The order had gone out for them to go to work in their uniforms and to take their rifles, ammunition and bayonets with them. During the sunshine of July and August, as we worked the fields together, these arms were always stashed close at hand. The talk centered on what they would do if German paratroopers landed in the grove, the five-acre plot of trees on the north east corner of the farm which gave it its name. They talked about how they would have to kill by hand once they ran out of ammunition. With the frequent bombs in Norwich and worries of invasion, it was an exciting and frightening summer. As I lay in bed I would mull over my conversations with the farmhands. I no longer fancied myself a David-killing Goliath, but the fact that Mother was praying for us still seemed sufficient protection against any possible calamity.

A busload of London evacuees arrived in the village that summer, which helped take our minds off grander matters. These evacuees were mostly around my age, and came to stay with families who had extra bedrooms in their cottages and council houses. They themselves were an invading force as far as my village friends and Ivan and I were concerned. The boys amongst them were all over the place, having no idea of what a farm was about. They chased ducks, stoned cows, trampled the grain in the fields, shouted at horses that we would be driving and, as far as we were concerned, were making a general nuisance of themselves. With a common enemy to fight, the village boys, Ivan and I banded together and called ourselves the Diamond Gang. Setting up a hideout inside an overgrown hedge, we furnished it with our own precious object—a stone shaped like a diamond that we found in the Beck. It was kept in an Oxo tin hidden in the trunk of a dead tree. The Londoners had heard of this treasure and threatened to steal it, so we had something to fight for. There were plenty of small clods to use as ammunition on the freshly harrowed field. We had amassed piles of them just the right size around the outside of our cave, so from whichever direction the attack came we would have plenty of ammunition, not unlike the Home Guard.

    The battle broke out on the edge of the low meadow on our farm, near the Beck. We knew we were good at throwing clods and stones: we'd spent lots of time on target practice and had the advantage of being on home terrain. But our antagonists were fast learners. They also outnumbered us: there were about seven of us and eight or nine of them. We beat them, but I became a casualty. During the heat of battle of what became almost hand to hand fighting, I had a clod hit me between the legs. I couldn't get up. I think my screams did more than anything to end the conflict. The London boys took to their heels and ran.

    Easing myself up from the place I'd fallen I went home with my hand held gently over the painful wound. Mother was on the back lawn talking with one of the circuit ministers, who happened to be visiting that afternoon. I was crying and she came over to me. "What on earth is the matter?" she asked while she looked me over quickly for signs of blood. "I got hit in the balls with a clod." That did it. She forgot my injury and lit into me for speech like that, especially in front of a minister. He didn't look so shocked. In fact, I detected a quick smile on his face. If nothing else, the incident made it abundantly clear why the Germans must never be allowed to land on our soil. It would take more than clods from a freshly seeded field of wheat to protect our balls and everything else. I prayed that God would never let it happen.

    After the summer's excitement as the school year resumed, the attractions of Bracondale could hardly compete. In all subjects except geography, in which I had my war maps to aid me, and algebra, which for some reason I took to, I was proving to be a less-than-stellar student. Homework was my biggest burden. To think that a perfectly good evening had to be spoiled by the two hours of study we were supposed to do. There were usually tests the next day on anything that had been read the evening before and I would regularly be in trouble. If I did manage to pass it was by talking with a classmate about the reading and extracting as much information as possible just prior to the test.

The fact that schoolwork had become harder was not the only reason I found it difficult to concentrate. I had started to hatch and rear chickens at home, and I had a small garden for lettuce, radish, cress and red beet. I was also becoming interested in astronomy, thanks to a telescope that my parents had bought me. With the aid of a tripod made out of three broom sticks and parts of a Meccano set, I could make the necessary adjustments to the lens. I would spend hours outside on warm dark evenings looking at the stars and planets.

At the same time, in those early war years, I gained several new school friends. Wally Hemmant was in the class ahead of me. I was drawn by his vulnerability: he seemed to be lonely and longing for a friend. We would sit together chatting for hours in the playground between classes and at break. I did most of the talking, trying my best to impress him with my fantasizing; my exaggerations about my home, family, our possessions and the chapel; and my thoughts and theories about God and the world in general. But Wally's position in the class ahead of me affected our friendship and I found myself growing closer to Colin Carver, who was in my class. The son of a fruit farmer at Hellington Corner, he started coming over to the house on half days and then for weekends. We called him Kipper, meaning "half a head and no guts"—one of those opposite nicknames because he was very clever and, though small, could defend himself against anyone. He began coming to our Sunday school as well. He had a wry wit, which showed itself in all things, including chapel services. In an autograph book I have kept from my schooldays his is one of the most memorable entries:

Some go to church just for a walk
Some go to church just for a talk
Some go there to sleep and nod,
But few go there to worship God.

Colin was good at athletics. We competed fiercely through all our remaining time at school. On sports day, held in June every year, the whole school, junior and senior, went to the Lakenham cricket ground to compete in running and to present Sergeant's gym and marching display to our parents. In 1941 my parents were on the edge of the field with all the others. I ran my first race of the day and won. I came back to tell them. Father laughed and said he thought I was the one lumbering along behind all the others. That was McCartney and he was useless at sports. Father's remark cut deep. It caused me to go into one of my sulky silences, my initial way of dealing with any bitter emotion. It made me determined to show him that I was the best runner and jumper in my age group. I won most of my races that day and did well in the long jump.

By the summer of 1941, I was twelve, and was expected to do a full day's work on the farm. I was now ready to handle a wide range of jobs: getting the cows in from the meadow each afternoon, stacking the sheaves while the corn was being reaped, loading the corn into carts, driving the horses with loads of sheaves from the field to the stack yard, and on rainy days mucking about in the cow yard and calf stalls, helping to cut wood, and clipping the hedges around the lawns and the orchard. Father could find jobs galore, and he never liked to see us sitting down. He said he would pay me as he had payed Ivan for the last two summers. Despite the terrible events of those months in Britain and elsewhere, it was for us a happy, healthy summer. Mother often reminded us that there were people in Britain who were hungry and that we should be happy to have so much. We were.

I continued dabbling in my homegrown business. By this time I had bantams, rabbits and a few hens. Mr. Seppings, the village butcher, was always on the lookout for locally produced food, and the idea occurred to me that I should buy an incubator and hatch larger numbers of chicks, selling them in about ten weeks when they were large enough for Mr. Seppings. I saved my money and bought an old incubator from a poultry farm in the next village. It could hatch seventy eggs at a time. Meanwhile, as 1941 neared its end, there occurred half a world away an event that would profoundly affect us: Pearl Harbour. The Americans were finally in the war, and their servicemen would be on the way as soon as the necessary preparations were made for their arrival.

After Bracondale's Sports Day, 1941. Lovewell family collection.

Evidence of the impending influx came when a fleet of trucks began hauling gravel from all the old pits in the area, and from some new ones, to Seething and Hethel, villages close by where two air bases were being built. The word soon got around, "the Yanks are coming here." Runways were appearing in fields and woods, along with hangars, tool shops, sheds of every description, living quarters, kitchens, dining rooms, cinemas—buildings, buildings, buildings. Heavy tractors, bulldozers and earth removers disturbed the Norfolk quiet until the men and equipment came.

Once they appeared, their trucks could be seen and heard everywhere: on the village lanes and in the city streets. The hordes of gum-chewing men who filled them were willing to talk to anyone and had an inexhaustible supply of candy and gum to hand out. All at once there was the incessant noise of engines being revved up and planes taking off and landing: the bedlam of war was overhead and in our ears. I loved it.

We soon got to know the tail markings of the Liberator bombers at the two nearby airfields. We could count them in the mornings just as we left for school when they were taking off for a bombing raid, which seemed to be just about every day from then on. They would circle higher and higher over the villages until they were in tight formation and then they would head out over the North Sea for their missions of death. We would count them on their return. Often not as many flew back as went out, and sometimes so very few returned. We would spot bombers limping home with an engine stopped or a piece of tail shot off. Mother didn't like to watch them coming back to the airfield and she shushed any sign of us talking or laughing about seeing planes badly shot up. There were boys in those planes, she said, with parents worrying and praying for them.

We would see the airmen in Norwich on their times off. Smartly uniformed, they were impossible to miss with their loud shouting and raucous laughter, a whistle for any girl, and money galore. They courted, walked, drank and sometimes fought. They even attempted bicycling. It was clear they couldn't care less, and given the odds of imminent death they lived under it was not hard to understand why.

One morning in May 1942 we cycled to school as usual. Ivan and I had just over a mile to pedal by ourselves. A nearby neighbour, Timmy Mills, would then join us and after another mile Roy Harold made a foursome. We enjoyed the freedom of the ride every day and cared little about the weather, though if it was continual rain or the roads were snow-covered or icy we would take a bus. We were all farmers' sons. Roy's father had died a few years before, and Roy's mother was managing the farm, which seemed very strange to the farm men and others, including ourselves.

We were never short of conversation, always talking and laughing together. That day when we arrived at the top of Bracondale Hill and the school came into view, we saw something out of the ordinary. There were fire engines outside the junior school and police and air wardens stood about. In the previous night's air raid, the school had taken a direct hit. There had been a death—Muirhead, the head boy of Bracondale and a boarder there during the week. It had been his turn for fire watching. He had been in the front porch of the junior school, almost directly under where the bomb had exploded.

On the other side of the road, the senior school had been hit by an incendiary bomb and was still smouldering. Only one of its classrooms had been burned, but there was water and smoke damage everywhere. The word got out from one of the staff that there would be no school until further notice. Unforgivably forgetting about Muirhead's fate, we let out a great whoop and rode off home for our enforced holiday. Afterwards, though, his death haunted me. Many were getting killed. Now I knew one of them. Not very well, but I had seen him every day at school. Death. The end? The beginning? In chapel it was spoken of as a beginning, nothing to fear, but as this death hit me, I had my doubts.

Not too long after that we were in chapel one Sunday afternoon. Ivan, Tommy Nicholson and I were sitting on the back pew, a place we'd claimed as our own once our parents allowed us to sit where we wanted. The service was almost over, the sermon had concluded, and the preacher was giving out the last hymn. He stopped as a plane thundered overhead at treetop level. My cousin Mary, who was not in chapel, but outside nearby, remembers seeing several American airmen running inside the plane and one at the door preparing to jump with no parachute. There was an explosion and then silence. People went white and I felt sick.

David E. Lovewell

There was no last hymn, just a benediction with mention of the airmen on the plane. Ivan, Tommy and I ran from the chapel and looked to the east where black smoke was billowing and small explosions could still be heard.

We raced across the fields to where the plane had crashed. En route we had to climb through some barbed wire. I had on a new Sunday suit, and heard the horrible noise of my pant leg being ripped open on the spiked wire. What would Mother say now? Somehow it didn't matter with the plane just a few hundred yards ahead in flames. Before us one of the airmen lay dead, face up, staring straight into the sky. We stopped and looked. One of the Yankee ground crewmen who often stayed with us, Andy Knox, had been attending chapel as well. He had followed us out the door and now came running up behind us. He too stared. I had never seen a dead man before. I felt cold inside, a kind of sickly cold.

Andy said, "O my God." I looked at his eyes and he was crying. A lump came to my throat. Andy said, "This is war; this is what war does." He wasn't talking to me, he was talking to himself. He never wanted to be in the war anyway; we had gathered that from his conversation. His heart was in Missouri on his father's farm that he was always talking about. I thought of my uncles and for a brief moment I knew why they never answered my question about killing Germans. If they had done any killing it was not to be spoken of. From that time on the war wasn't fun; it wasn't anything to laugh about. Mother was right. God meant us to live in peace. The war had come right on our farm. During the months that followed, and for the remainder of the war, I started to pray that it would finish, my spirits no longer as carefree as they had been in previous years.

When I returned to school in September of 1942 after another summer's work on the farm, I was about to make another friend. Sitting next to me in third form was a Norwich boy, Colin Riches. I needed Colin. He read through the homework we were assigned and was willing to share his precious knowledge with me before tests. Occasionally when I was stumped by a question he would make little signs to help me out. One has stayed with me. Where was Napoleon exiled? He kept pointing at his elbow. Of course, the Isle of Elba! I began spending time with Colin and a friend of his named Peter Porter in the playground and after lunch. One of my ways of showing friendship was to ask people home. Colin wanted to see the farm and I knew Mother was always good for a meal. I asked him over one Saturday. I remember Colin's words to her as he was leaving to cycle back to Norwich. "I have had a most pleasurable time with your hospitality." This charming language duly impressed her, and I knew I could ask him again without difficulty. That meant that two Colins were now frequent visitors to Grove Farm.

With Beryl and Ivan, 1944.
Lovewell family collection.

The end of the school year saw Colin Riches with a whole summer in front of him in the city and nothing particular to do. Again I boldly made a suggestion, this time that he come and work on the farm for eight weeks. Father was short of labour and jumped at the idea, while Mother visited Mr. and Mrs. Riches, just to see what these good people were like, given that Colin was such a polite and well-spoken boy. So Colin came and helped get the harvest in.

We used horses and he first had to overcome his nervousness with those large, powerful and sometimes headstrong farm workers. One of his early jobs was driving loaded wagons by himself from the grain fields to the stack yards and then back again once the wagons had been emptied. He must have had some frightening times. We were used to the beasts and never thought anything about handling them, but Colin was from the city.

He slept in the bedroom with me. The first night after using the horses, and for a number of nights following, he jumped up from the bed in the middle of the night shouting "Whoa, Whoa!" The first time it scared the wits out of me, but his night horses soon became a joke. Colin returned summer after summer, becoming a surrogate member of the family. He would occasionally visit during the winter months as well.

And in those years Colin was by no means the only one who made Grove Farm a second home. Throughout my boyhood, the house had been divided into two parts, our immediate family living on one side, my paternal grandparents on the other. I didn't really know my grandfather George Lovewell: he died when I was five. A tall man, serious-minded and athletic, he made his mark as an ambitious farmer. In the 1870s he had moved to Hill Farm with his father William, a market gardener, from the Norfolk village of Kirstead not far from Shotesham. First the father and then the son rented portions of both Hill Farm and Grove Farm from the Fellowes family, and by the early years of the century my grandfather was living at Grove Farm. In 1920 when the Fellowes family found it necessary to auction off the bulk of their estate, as so many landowners did at that time, my grandfather scooped up both Grove Farm and Hill Farm for the princely sums of £2200 and £3050.

After he died, my grandmother continued living on her side of the farmhouse. During the worst days of the bombing of Norwich, my uncle Stanley and his wife Jane, Father's sister, were bombed out of their home and came with their offspring John and Myrtle to live with her. On our side of the house we had a cousin, John Dutton-Briant. Son of my uncle Bernard, the tank corps captain in World War I who became a wealthy Brighton estate

Grove Farm 1944 (from left to right): Myrtle Sutton, Christopher Gregory, Colin Carver, Charlie Watling, Tommy Nicholson, Flossie Clark, Alfred Lovewell, John Dutton-Briant, Ivan, Jane Sutton, the author, Stanley Sutton, Ernest Lovewell, Gladys Lovewell, Melva Carver, Beryl, Olive Carver, Mrs. Carver, Mr. Atoe. Lovewell family collection.

agent and married Father's sister, John was with us for far longer than originally planned, staying well after the war's end until he left for boarding school. During the years when Norwich was bombed we had others staying near us as well. Mr. Gregory, our optician in the city, parked a trailer on the front lawn where he passed the nights, and where his family lived more or less fulltime. Soon after, an associate of Mr. Gregory's moved his own family to a trailer on the front meadow across from the farmhouse. And there were other more occasional visitors: American ground crew from the nearby airbases, offspring of friends of Mother's from her early Norwich days, and, later on, just after the liberation of Europe, several boys from Holland. If one also adds in Lily Peg and her husband Arthur, our cowman, who lived in a cottage on the farm, there must often have been close to twenty people passing the night on the premises. This was not a circumstance that I gave much thought to at the time, but it was something that both my parents, as well as our adult visitors, must have been fully aware of. On Sundays, the house would become even more populated. Colin Carver was now permanently attached to our chapel. He came each Sunday morning and stayed for the day, while his sisters Melva and Olive, and often their mother, would join him for the evening service as well. Thanks to Mr. Gregory, we have a photograph of one of these Sundays, with most of those staying at the house as well as several other Sunday visitors.[1]

For me this image captures a key feature of the farm in those years: the fact that my parents and grandmother, but especially the former, were able to turn the farm into a refuge for so many during the long years of the war. This generosity was by no means unique: countless British families were doing similar things. But that doesn't detract from the tremendous significance of what my parents accomplished by doing this. It endures as a fitting emblem of the deep faith and commitment to others they exhibited throughout their lives. By 1944, of course, the outlook of the war was far different than it had been just a year or two earlier, but the practical threats we faced were as real as ever. In those last years of the war the Germans boasted about the secret weapons they claimed would assure them victory—the V1 and V2 bombs. The V1 was the first to appear. Known to us as the doodlebug, it was a noisy flying machine that travelled as fast as our fighters. It could be heard approaching for some time before it was overhead. We soon learned to listen for the cutting out of the engine, which meant immediate descent and explosion when it reached the ground. A few buzzed over the village both in the day and at night, but none ever landed nearby.

---

1 The others in the photo are my parents' friend Charlie Watling, a friend of Melva's named Flossie Clark, our neighbour and Ivan's friend Tommy Nicholson, the lay preacher for that Sunday named Mr. Atoe, Father's brother Uncle Alfred, and Mr. Gregory's young son Christopher.

A Place in the Sun

The V2s were different altogether. They gave no warning of their approach until the deadly moment they hit the ground. My own experience with them was limited to one event which occurred in early October of 1944. The whole working force of the farm had gathered one morning to thresh a stack of wheat at the back of our house. The morning was cold and clear. Literally out of the blue there was an enormous boom. I felt the blast of air and heard the thud of shrapnel. Looking towards the village church, I could see flames, billowing smoke and branches flying through the air, though the V2's landing point was shrouded by trees. Strangely enough we all carried on with our work, talking about what had happened but not running to see if there was call for our help. Mother went down to the village and found out that no one was hurt. The bomb had dropped in a marshy area near the rectory.

We got to know three members of American ground crews well. The first was Murphy, from a small town in Maine. He was drawn to our family, staying often with Grandma and Grandpa Black, who by this time were living in a cottage tucked away on one of the farm fields, and he occasionally came over to the farmhouse for meals. His presence was welcomed by all of us, me in particular, for he was a guitarist with a wide repertoire of gospel songs known by heart, many of them completely new to us. Whenever he was in Shotesham he would accompany Grandpa Black to his various preaching appointments, bringing his guitar and offering to sing. How I loved these impromptu performances when he played at the chapel, the most beautiful music I'd ever heard.

Murphy had an enormous appetite, which he exhibited whenever he joined us for a meal. To our amazement, he would happily twin jam with celery, marmalade with bacon, and jellies with meats, in what for us were breathtakingly extravagant amounts. We had long been conditioned to spread just a little jam on our thinly buttered bread. Murphy would take two or three spoonful and pile the jam into a dish to eat it without even bothering to spread it on a slice. It was my first acquaintance with Yankee mores—not just their lack of self-consciousness and their spontaneity, even with strangers, but this willingness to satisfy a whim with a debonair air unimaginable to a proper English family such as us.

Once the meals were finished and the washing up done Murphy would get out his guitar and sing yet more gospel songs cowboy style. He always had my complete attention. If only I could play and sing like that. I persuaded Mother that I needed a guitar and was allowed to buy one with my chicken money. Murphy would sit for hours teaching me the necessary chords to strum his songs. For a while he had me play with him in the chapel services. That was heaven indeed. But I never mastered the art, and pretty well gave up after Murphy returned to the States.

The second of our Yankee visitors was Andy Knox, who had been with us in chapel when the plane crashed on our farm. Though he lacked Murphy's easy charisma and charm, he developed a close rapport with our entire family, as evidenced by the fact that of all three of our Yankee regulars he was the only one we called by his first name. His farm background helped, but so did his thoughtfulness—he was older than the other two and fully aware of his surroundings. On one occasion when both Murphy and he were eating with us, I remember Murphy engaged in one of his displays of jam consumption. Andy immediately reprimanded him. "Remember these people are on rations." After that, Murphy was more careful at our table.

My own friendship with Andy had a memorable result. He had a niece in his Missouri home town, Arleen Paynter, who wanted a British pen pal. Andy considered me a suitable candidate and so Arleen and I started to write. We exchanged pictures and I thought, as I had with the few passing crushes before this, "the most beautiful girl in the world!" And since Arleen was American and I had become fascinated by all things American she headed my list of infatuations. I longed for the post—we wrote about once a month—and I read, re-read and read again her treasured letters. For a charmed year or so near the end of the war all other girls faded. Arleen took up my dream time and brightened my whole horizon. Alas, the two of us lost contact, leaving little but those glowing dreams.

Our third Yankee regular was named Pulfis. A chef on the base, he introduced us to American dishes such as lemon meringue pie, which in our eyes was a magical concoction, especially eaten fresh and hot whenever he baked one in our own kitchen. Though never guessed by the rest of the family, he brought another piece of foreign culture with him as well. I had noticed that he always paid me special interest whenever he visited the farmhouse. On one occasion, I and the rest of the chapel's Sunday school pupils were invited for a tour of the base where Pulfis and Andy were stationed. Pulfis arranged matters so that he could give me a private tour of the storerooms behind the mess hall. Once we were alone, he blurted out the fact that he was in love with me and attempted a hurried kiss. My entire knowledge of homosexuality being limited to the Bible's few infamous references, I was utterly appalled. As usual, my gift of the gab sufficed to get me out of the storeroom in short order and I made certain the two of us were never alone together again. Still, I decided that Pulfis's life was probably difficult enough without me adding to his troubles with idle talk. From then on I viewed him more with pity than disdain, while his attentions added to my understanding of just how exotic our Yankee guests were. I for one would not soon forget any of them and I am sure that the fascination with American culture that I gained in those years, first with Murphy and Andy and then with Arleen, helped in some subliminal way to drive the wanderlust that would ultimately see me pass the bulk of my life as a North American.

In the meantime, all of us were waiting impatiently for the tables to turn with an allied invasion of the continent. When D-Day finally did arrive, cool and wet, I was spending what would be my last weeks attending Bracondale. The first lesson that day was a French class with Monsieur Vincent, who had escaped from France in a small boat with his family at the time of Dunkirk. He had been at our school ever since. The news from across the Channel began filtering through on the early BBC news and when we got to school it was being talked about by everyone. Monsieur Vincent discarded that day's material for an impromptu lesson in geography on the area of France that was his home—Normandy. We had never seen him so excited and yet so concerned. There was the possibility of freedom now for his country, but he had family still living there. His anxiety for them was obvious. "Mon Dieu! Mon Dieu! This bloody war!"

As for me, I had already made a decision to leave school for good and begin full-time work on the farm. This was one year after Ivan had decided the same thing. Despite my growing interest in the ministry, this seemed the natural thing to do, partly because I was at the common school-leaving age, and partly because I knew Father was facing a shortage of workers. If Mother had any reservations about my decision, I don't remember her voicing them. And in retrospect, it's likely that by this time Bracondale had provided me with all that it could.

The end of 1944 saw the Battle of the Bulge in the Ardennes, as the Germans made one last great stand and pushed back the allies. What did Hitler have up his sleeve to reverse the course of the war so dramatically? Was there some secret weapon he was making time for that would give him victory so near to what appeared to be the end? The news on Christmas Day particularly worried me. I asked one of my uncles, Stanley, about the bleak outlook. He seemed surprised by my pessimism. This was just one final struggle, he said, the throes of a dying country. To see my uncle so confident encouraged me. Perhaps we really could begin to dream of the victorious end of what felt like an ever-present struggle.

A Place in the Sun

And my uncle was right, except for a terrible event for him and his family that left its mark on all of us. Stanley and Jane's son John was two years older than Ivan, outgoing, playful and knowledgeable, and had what in our eyes appeared to be an enviable patina of city sophistication. Especially during the years he lived with his family on the farm, we got to know him well. As soon as he was old enough to sign up, he did, and began training as a Fleet Air Arm pilot. These spots were much coveted by new recruits, and the fact that John had nabbed one suitably impressed us. But of course there were worries as well, and it was those worries that were to prove all too real.

One night in early March 1945 my aunt and uncle had accompanied Mother to a meeting at the rectory with the new vicar. While they were away from the house, a village policeman arrived at our door. Father, Ivan and I were there to hear the news: John had crashed during a practice landing on an aircraft carrier and died instantly. Under no circumstance should his coffin be open at the funeral. The policeman stayed to tell my aunt and uncle in person. By the time they and Mother returned from the rectory it was late. Ivan and I were upstairs in bed, but we heard the sounds from the sitting room below. I will never forget listening in the darkness to the loud cry of anguish "Oh John" which my aunt let out after the muffled words of the policeman. Years later, John's sister Myrtle told us that after her mother's death, when Myrtle was cleaning out my aunt and uncle's home, she found John's uniform that the navy had sent back carefully folded in a bedroom drawer. For my aunt and uncle, the grief of that night turned into a lifelong sense of loss from which they, and we, never completely recovered.

Adding to the difficulty in accepting John's death was the fact that it had occurred as the war was already winding down. By the spring of 1945 the fighting in Europe seemed to be ebbing away in the same gradual way it had begun. Just as there had been much talk of fighting before the war started, now there was much talk of the coming peace. As VE Day approached, it was decided there would be a bonfire and village dance on the Common. For weeks we collected garbage, wood, old tires, and brush from the farms until we had a giant pile that, once fired, could be seen for miles around: something like the fires that the bombing had caused earlier in the war, but a fire we could dance and sing around with no more fear of bombs, doodlebugs or V2 rockets.

That night the villagers gathered at dusk. A man named Nicky Notley had been selected as honorary fire-lighter. He had joined the Territorial Army in the mid-1930s and had swaggered his way first through peace and then the war, surviving front-line service, imprisonment and escape without a scratch. Before the war he had managed to escape all forms of work without any visible shortage of money and it was suspected that somehow or other he would have managed to avoid most hardships during the war as well. He had now returned just in time for some self-induced glory. But he was the only hero we had. Besides, who knew what trials he might actually have suffered as he sailed past potential disasters without injury? Decked out in the full private's uniform of khaki, topped with a beret, he was our star for the evening.

We waited for darkness to descend before starting the lighting ceremony. In the interim there was much light-heartedness and joking, most directed at Nicky, which he took in good spirits, as a few dignitaries huddled in a little group separate from the main crowd as though they were the ones we'd gathered to thank. Eventually Nicky left to join them with much shouting and cat-calling from the rest of us on when and how the fire should be lit. A large can of kerosene stood innocently by the pile of rubbish.

The long awaited moment arrived. Nicky took up the can, unscrewed its stopper and poured out its contents on the edge of the pile. In all the excitement, he must have spilled some on himself because the instant he struck his cigarette lighter it was Nicky who was on fire. A great round of laughter went up as Nicky danced and shouted for help while the village elders scurried around in a panic and everyone gave instructions to extinguish the blaze. Finally he was smothered with someone's Home Guard overcoat. He'd burned his hands slightly and his hair was a little singed but he had no serious burns and nothing was going to stop him carrying out his ceremonial task. He again boldly put his lighter to the kerosene-soaked rubbish which flashed into flame. By now the actual bonfire was an anticlimax. We'd had our fun seeing Nicky blazing like a victory torch for those few brief moments. There was a strange kind of satisfaction for everyone in this since Nicky had always been a braggart and show-off with his ever growing stories and his peacock-strutting ways. His comeuppance had been in front of everyone and somehow the books were balanced.

After the bonfire came a round of speeches and dancing at the village hall. Major Fellowes stressed there was no need to single out heroes for special commendation. Every person in Britain, man, woman and child, had done their part. We were all heroes. People looked at each other, smiled and nodded in agreement. But then a village elder rose and said we had good reason to celebrate like this but the war wasn't over yet. There were still the Japanese to finish off, and we had one village lad in a Japanese prisoner of war camp. The final war celebrations could not be held until George Harmer was back home. We were all silent. Everyone had noticed that the Harmers and the family of George's wife, the Nicholsons, had not been with us that night. They were waiting and praying for George's return.

Once the crowd dispersed and each of the villagers made their way home, Ivan and I ran ahead and switched on every light in the house. No more blackouts. No more air raids. The nights could now be ablaze without anyone shouting, "Put that bloody light out!"

The rest of the war seemed so far away. I still followed its progress each day on the BBC radio news, but I found it harder to picture what was happening in the various Pacific islands whose names were so unfamiliar. The only real remaining part of the war was the remembered face of George Harmer, who might be out there somewhere still alive, if we were lucky. He was named in our prayers and often mentioned at chapel services.

The war's ultimate end arrived abruptly. The atomic bomb became the subject of much speculation. Villagers were saying that we would have to find a way of settling international disputes without violence. War had at last become impossible with such a weapon, for now it meant total destruction. The whole world was at stake, not just a house or a school or a city. We were entering the longed for peace with a greater fear to haunt us.

The VJ Day celebrations did not involve a bonfire. The last performance could never be repeated. We made do with a dance and speeches in the village hall, but this time there was a sense of incompleteness in the festivities—there was still no word of George and his fate. Afterwards Ivan and I went home and took a pair of twelve-gauge double barrel shot guns, loaded them and carried them outside the back door and each fired four shots into the air in rapid succession. At the time we didn't really know why, though in retrospect I suppose it was our own way to mark the hope that no more shots would need to be fired in anger. We looked forward to the end of rationing, the getting on with farming and being able to drive about with no restrictions on our movement. Peace was a new experience after such a long, long war. And if George Harmer returned from the Far East there would be no more fresh bouts of war sadness.

The first word from him since his capture from Singapore arrived soon after VJ Day. He was alive and would be coming back. After several months, he did return, being driven straight to the house of his wife's family, the Nicholsons. A large sign welcoming him was strung up to greet him. When he finally appeared from the house to acknowledge those of us who had gathered there, we did not recognize him. He was painfully thin, his skin yellow, and though he was all smiles it was not the same smile he had on leaving years before. Recovering that smile would be slow work.

Whatever George had seen or heard or felt he never told us. It was his secret and it seemed he was trying to forget it by his silence. We didn't ask, though we saw and felt his lingering anguish. Now that he was back in the village, his wounds healed, but slowly.

At All Saints Church there was a service of thanksgiving. Coming out afterwards people stood about talking in the elm-shaded churchyard. Someone drew attention to where the V2 rocket had exploded in the trees a few hundred yards away. The hole had filled with water, creating another village pond. "I was down there this morning. Would you believe it, a water-hen has already used it to hatch its chicks." Peace had returned.

And for me there was a new girl on the horizon. Near the end of the war our Dutch guests came over to live with us from Rotterdam after its liberation. These boys were skinny and unruly, but I so enjoyed their company. It was a novel experience being with people my own age who spoke another language. The boy I got to know best was named Gerhard Breetfelt. His sister Nelly was too old for the travel program and stayed in Holland. But Gerhard got us writing. Again, her photograph bowled me over and I forgot all about Arleen and her predecessors. Another sun was beaming down on me. In 1946 I travelled to Holland to visit Gerhard's family for a week and there was Nelly in person. I soon realized that she was a sophisticated city girl whose interests in boys went far beyond me on her local scene. Here I had done nothing but think of her for months on end while, as I started to realize, she had played a wider field than was imaginable in my experience. That was a shock, but I did my best to accept this setback with equanimity and when I returned home she and I continued to write. In any case by this time I had more important things to think about. There was the small matter of my future.

Chapter 4: New Horizons

From early boyhood I had dreams of being a minister. That meant a Methodist minister, for Methodism was the only church I knew until my teens. And as far as the rest of the family was concerned, there was no question about this either. On Sunday afternoons in front of the fire in our sitting room, I would sometimes have the chance to play the role of preacher. Beryl would be at the piano serving as the organist, and my parents—sometimes Ivan as well, if he could be persuaded—would be the congregation. A hymn or two would be sung, and I would give a brief homily, no doubt inspired by whatever words had been delivered at the most recent chapel service. Aided and abetted by my mother, who often told me of her dream that I would choose this as my vocation, I was following the appointed path.

It was in the dying months of the war that my youthful visions began to coalesce into definite plans, as I became intensely interested in my spiritual heritage and journey. I had regularly heard preachers urge the practice of daily prayer and Bible readings, and the models were also there in my own family. Both my parents would kneel by their beds before turning in for the night and again on rising in the morning. Father did his reading each evening. After tea he might spend a little time with the Norfolk paper but always he would pick up his Schofield Bible and read with knit eyebrows, serious face and ardent concentration. Then he would disappear for half an hour or so. I knew he used this time to have a final look around the sheds and barns, checking on the animals, doors and gates.

One night I discovered what else he was doing during these disappearances. I happened to go outside looking for something when I tried the door of the beet shed. It was locked. That seemed strange. I gave it some hard yanks until he opened it, unlatching it from the inside. With a flash I realized what he must have been doing: praying. I can't remember what I said but I do recall his embarrassment. Soon after, once he had left the shed, I returned. By a bag of chaff I could see where his elbows had been pressed while he knelt, and it was still warm. "When you pray," says the gospel, "go into your room and shut the door and pray to your Father who is in secret..." For him this was a command, and he had obeyed it secretly for a long time. Mother too was diligent in both Bible reading and prayer. She would read during the day, often in the afternoons, and there were always devotional books on her bedside table. She too must have prayed in secret, probably in her bedroom. But I never broke in on her unexpectedly.

Now I too started in earnest with prayer and Bible reading, and it took up much of my thought. At times it would be compulsive. I felt that if I didn't do it every day something might happen to me or to someone in my family. But gradually it became something I wanted to do as well. I followed carefully any suggestions I picked up from preachers at our services. So much emphasis was placed by all of them on personal devotions.

Our village chapel had been established as a part of New Connexion, a movement that seceded from the main branch of Methodism soon after the lifetime of the denomination's founder John Wesley. This break had occurred because of New Connexion's emphasis on the role of the laity in church governance, which at the time of the Napoleonic Wars was seen as all too likely to lead to political radicalism. That helps explain why the individual credited with bringing Methodism to the village was herself a layperson. In the late 1860s this woman, named Charlotte Bruce, started to travel from her home in the nearby village of Stoke Holy Cross to lead evangelical meetings on Shotesham Common.

Tradition has it that she and her husband differed on questions of religion. As a short history of Shotesham Chapel relates:

David E. Lovewell

Shotesham Chapel. © John Salmon.

> *There was an occasion when Mrs. Bruce was conducting a Christian meeting on the Common when she saw her husband, intent, she believed, to break up the meeting; this resourceful woman at once announced the hymn, 'Shall I for fear of feeble man The Spirit's course in me restrain Or, undismayed, in deed and word Be a true witness for my Lord.' It is said that Mr. Bruce at once retraced his steps with downcast head.[1]*

Mrs. Bruce finally moved to Shotesham and did so without her feeble husband in tow. In later decades, after the chapel was built in 1875, others gradually took over her role. Her successors included my grandparents, who often entertained the visiting lay preachers and ministers, hosted the chapel's annual picnics on Grove Farm's front meadow, and in my grandfather's case taught Sunday school. Mother in her turn became the chapel's leading

---
1 *100 Years of Methodist Witness, 1879-1979: Shotesham Methodist Church*, p. 1.

light, and in her usual way attracted others with her. This included her parents once they moved from the city as well as her sister Violet and Violet's husband Billy, a worker at the Norwich Coleman's factory. They too came to live in the village, Uncle Billy taking on the task of Sunday School teaching.

During the war, our family's link with the chapel was particularly intimate. Because the large blackout shutters that would have been needed to cover the chapel windows were so expensive, Sunday evening services were held instead in Grandma Lovewell's parlour. These proved popular, often with 30 or 40 people present. With all of us crammed in the domestic clutter of my grandmother's living quarters, the fire blazing in wintertime and Beryl accompanying our hymns on the family piano, there was camaraderie and warmth that, at least to my young eyes, made these times seem particularly special.

As the war neared its end, Ivan and I took on our own initiative in chapel affairs. By this time the elderly Reverend Fellowes had retired, and in his place was a much younger man, the Reverend Eric Geddes, who was eager to sweep away the clouds of tradition that for so long had clung to All Saints Church and its rectory. My parents, like other village Methodists, were keen to reciprocate his obvious desire to collaborate with us. When Ivan and I heard a radio program on Children's Hour about church youth groups, we mentioned to Mother our wish that we start a group for all the village boys. She suggested we visit the Reverend Geddes and tell him our plans. When we did, he was enthusiastic to help, especially since there was no Anglican Boys' Brigade in the village. Besides providing us with a place to meet—the loft room in the rectory's onetime carriage house—he helped us organize the group's first meetings. In classic English vicar style, Geddes cultivated a wide range of interests. He was a knowledgeable amateur astronomer and owned a powerful five-inch telescope, which was front and centre at many of our meetings whenever the skies were clear.

Meanwhile I'd already started the process of becoming a lay preacher, a necessary step for candidature to the Methodist ministry, though I hadn't known it at that time. It required acceptance to an initial stage of training known as being on note, which meant I accompanied senior lay preachers to various points in our fourteen-church circuit and was given the chance to take part in services. My name was presented to our circuit's central board, and I was approved for this stage, which lasted a year. My name was then brought up again and I graduated to being on trial. Now I was taking full services on my own while being scheduled in the quarterly plan of the circuit, so that I was responsible for designated Sundays at various chapels.

I was to gain a personal spiritual mentor as well—someone who was to have a major effect on my beliefs and evolving plans. His name was Alan Fisher, and he was the son of one of my mother's friends from her years growing up in Norwich. After moving to Shotesham, Mother had maintained a close relationship with Mrs. Fisher and her entire family. This continued after Mrs. Fisher's death, as Alan and his siblings continued to visit the farm. He had enlisted in the Royal Air Force medical corps. Late in the war he was involved in an air crash. Though he managed to escape without serious physical injury, he was trapped for some time in the burning plane. He was so shaken by the experience that he took an extended sick leave, most of which he spent with us. Having been brought up in Norwich's Surrey Chapel, whose strict literalist congregation had included Mother during her teens, Alan's whole life centred on his faith. We were soon sharing our thoughts and experiences, and he took me in hand as my self-appointed advisor.

He had friends in London who were part of an evangelical youth movement called the Young Life Campaign. Started in America, and still very much alive in its home country today, this movement had a large British chapter. Once the war was over I took several trips to London with Alan, staying with him in a

Christian guest house as we attended Young Life's huge rallies. These were exciting days. I was caught up in the enthusiasm of this movement and my friendship with Alan. His influence on me was so deep and his emphasis on personal devotions so strong that what I had started on my own was being reinforced and broadened more quickly than I might ever have imagined.

Even as I write the feelings of that period come washing through me again. It was such a straightforward and uncomplicated time. Every question seemed to have an answer. God was in heaven, the war was over, my own life stretched ahead of me with myriad possibilities, and things seemed to be unfolding as they should. I was being carried along by something bigger than myself and I relished it. In December 1946, this period of transition and discovery was capped with my baptism by immersion in Surrey Chapel. Also baptized that day was my school friend Colin Carver. It was an event that ensured I was following in my parents' footsteps. They had both been baptized at Surrey Chapel as adults, and they were there to witness my own rite of spiritual passage.

It was around this time that I plucked up courage to speak to the head minister of the circuit, Reverend Fred Doar, about the possibility of taking up the ministry as a career. His first response shook me. "Don't become a minister if you can help it." I almost gave up there and then: his answer felt like a rejection. But after weeks or months, I don't remember quite how long, I went to him again and told him that I really was serious. I found out later that this was his initial response to all those who came to him with such an enquiry. Later he would say to me, perhaps to explain his initial reaction: "If God wants you to be a minister, you won't be able to resist it, and if you become a minister without that call you won't be able to stand it."

I had begun studying by correspondence, with separate courses in the Old Testament and New Testament as well as in more theoretical subjects: theology and the study of rhetoric in the Bible, known as homiletics. In many ways, this was a fresh start to my education. Instead of the apathy I had exhibited during so much of my schooling, I was now a keen learner, driven by dreams of a career as well as the optimism born of my deepening beliefs. Still, I needed coaching. I was taken in hand by Fred Doar, who supervised my studies. Each week I would go to his office in Norwich to review my weekly assignments in each of my subjects.

This period was formative for my thinking about the ministry and my personal faith, a time for gradually shaping possible paths for the future. There were other young men in the circuit who were on a similar journey, displaying the same kind of interest about their faith as I was feeling. I discovered that Fred Doar was speaking with each of us individually for some time and then started to get us together once a week for discussion and study. He would assign us books to read and got each of us to preach a sermon for him at Chapel Field Road, the main church in our circuit.

As I pursued my studies I was faced with a whole new way of looking at the Bible. My parents were literalists, fundamentalists. Alan Fisher, too, was of this approach. He was militantly against the more liberal path being taken by the Methodist Church in its study programs for the laity and for ministerial candidates in its colleges. Alan did not approve of my leaving the path of scriptural orthodoxy or trampling about in the broad fields of heresy.

I had several emotional discussions with my parents, with Mother in particular expressing her keen disappointment that I should be duped into questioning the unerring truth of God's written word. But that was the end of the matter as far as explicit discussion with them was concerned: I learned to keep my own views on biblical interpretation to myself. With Alan it was more difficult to mask our differences, but we managed to maintain our friendship. In any case, the time soon came for me to start my formal training. When deciding among the various Methodist colleges in the country, I had taken Fred Doar's advice and applied

A Place in the Sun

to Handsworth in Birmingham. Living in the Midlands would be far different from what I was used to in Norfolk, though Birmingham was only a day's journey away on my newly purchased motorbike. As for Handsworth itself, my mentor assured me that it would provide all the mental and spiritual stimulation I would need, now that I knew my path.

First came a pre-collegiate year working as a candidate minister—a delay caused by the fact that so many were entering the Methodist ministry in the aftermath of the war. Between the summers of 1950 and 1951 I was posted not far from Birmingham in a circuit that encompassed a portion of the town of Stafford and a few nearby villages. That meant I found myself back in the sort of setting I was used to. I boarded at a private home called Pleasant View in the tiny village of Gnosall. Though there was another boarder next to me, I had my own private downstairs lounge and upstairs bedroom, and the house's owner, Miss Watkiss, insisted on bringing her delicious meals to me in my apartment. The arrangement suited me perfectly, as did the work I was expected to do, preaching twice a Sunday, sometimes in Gnosall, but also in the villages of Woodseaves and Eccleshall and at Rowley Street, one of the chapels in Stafford. My supervisor was Reverend Smith, a senior minister in the circuit with whom I felt especially comfortable. His prudent advice was a godsend, and I had a chance to see his stoicism in action the year I was there: after his wife died one Saturday evening he preached the very next morning as scheduled at Wesley, the largest church in the circuit.

Meanwhile it didn't take me long to make friends. I became close with May and Isaac Thompson, members of the Wesley congregation. When early in the spring of 1951 I visited their home at Rising Brook just outside Stafford for tea, among the other guests was a young woman from the nearby village of Penkridge. She was accompanied by her suitor at the time, a Methodist minister trainee already at Handsworth. The woman's name was Patricia Snelson. She was auburn-haired and pretty, with an easygoing manner and infectious laugh. It was a memorable meeting, though I was far less than pleased by the fact that she was with someone else, and found myself taking an immediate dislike to the man who was with her, my future Handsworth comrade.

But a few months later, Fate turned my way. In May, soon after I'd returned from a whirlwind trip to Norfolk to serve as best man at the wedding of Ivan and his longtime sweetheart Melva, I attended the annual Methodist Missionary Society garden party in Gnosall. It was a propitious day, for there on the chapel grounds with the Thompsons was none other than Pat, this time alone. As she and I chatted I was delighted to learn that her former suitor was no longer on the scene, and I proceeded to politely grill her about her life and background. Not only was she a Methodist, her father was a farmer, and it was clear from a few of her offhand comments that her background was a little more prosperous than mine. During the war, she'd attended a girls' boarding school named Hunmanby Hall that had been temporarily relocated to Lake Bassenthwaite in the Lake District. She had become a teacher, training in London before returning home to work in the Stafford area. She had just decided that teaching was not to her taste and was soon beginning a new round of training as a nurse.

At the party's end I asked her if she'd like to see my apartment at Miss Watkiss's. Pat came back with me to Pleasant View and I gave her a quick tour of my lounge. Reaching over to my tiny collection of books, I lent her one—a work by an American ne'er do well who'd gone to prison and discovered his faith while incarcerated. I've now forgotten the author's name, but I do remember the book's title—*Release*. Pat was not that interested in the book's contents, but when I phoned her a few days later to see if she'd started it (she was honest enough to say she hadn't) I asked her whether she would like to head out to the cinema in Stafford that weekend. She agreed.

From then on we were an item, though it's fair say that to begin with my enthusiasm outweighed hers. But she tolerated my

At Gnosall, Staffordshire. Lovewell family collection.

presence sufficiently to have me visit her family home. As always in these situations, her parents Cecily and Billy eyed me carefully. The fact that I was a Methodist was a plus, though truth be told Cecily would have preferred a young Methodist farmer with prospects over a minister in training like me. But the Snelsons' hospitality was genuine and their beautiful Regency farmhouse on the main road between Penkridge and Stafford was only a short motorbike ride away from Gnosall. I became a frequent visitor, while Pat and I headed out on road trips—first to the beauty spot Dovedale in Darbyshire, and soon after to Norfolk so she could meet my family. There a similar parental examination took place once we reached Grove Farm. Pat very quickly fell in love with Shotesham and my family.

Meanwhile my time at Gnosall was ending, and full-time studies in Birmingham beckoned. My mentor Fred Doar's prediction that I would enjoy Handsworth proved entirely correct. Being in the midst of a group of young men similar to myself, each at the same stage in our lives, was a boon. We all boarded at the

David E. Lovewell

Handsworth College, Birmingham. Courtesy John Houghton.

college and divided ourselves into groups called firms. These were made up of either three or four men; mine had three. I soon became very close with both my firm-mates Bernard Walkland and Ray Gibbon. Each of us had a separate apartment comprising a downstairs study with a fireplace and an upstairs bedroom. We ate communally in the college's dining room, and there was a central common room for special events and socializing, as well as a much-frequented library.

I loved this new existence. Though I had long ago accepted that I would never be an exceptional student, intellectual brilliance was not demanded at Handsworth. Instead we were expected to take both our studies and our future calling seriously—demands I could easily meet. Our classes centered on the classic subjects of ministerial training—biblical languages, homiletics, Old and New Testament studies, and theology—with professors who were acknowledged experts in their fields, most with national and some even international reputations. And these men were more than willing to provide individual attention and counsel when

Film Night at Handsworth. Lovewell family collection.

required. As students we were living in charmed surroundings, and we knew it.

The curriculum also included grounding of a more practical nature, with a memorable element that evoked the early days of Methodism, when preaching outdoors was the norm. Throughout our three years of study, we were expected to head out regularly to Birmingham's central square, the Bull Ring, where one of England's best known speaker's corners was located. Here, just next to a grim-looking statue of Lord Nelson, anyone could climb up on a podium and declaim to the crowd—in our case to speak about our Christian faith. This was no mean challenge. As a magnet for workers from all over the country and beyond, Birmingham gave its residents little choice but to adapt to its rough and tumble ways. The Bull Ring attracted the brashest of the locals, including a heavy sprinkling of those virulently opposed to religious belief of any sort.

The first few times I mounted the podium I was, quite frankly, terrified. My greenness to this exercise must have been abundantly

Bull Ring, Birmingham, circa 1950. From birmingham.gov.uk.

clear: on opening my mouth I faced a volley of heckling. Ignoring it was not an option: one quickly lost the crowd if one did. So I was forced to come up with on-the-spot retorts that deflected the verbal attacks, all the while keeping my ministerial cool. For all of my gift of the gab, this type of give and take was not a natural part of my repertoire. Luckily we had supporters in the crowd—not least Bryan Green, the Anglican canon of St. Martin's Church, just across the square. He would often come to listen and provide words of praise or sympathy afterwards, depending on our performance. We had a ready coach as well: a Handsworth student named Ray Billington who had a knack for Bull Ring speechifying and was always willing to provide practical pointers: "David, why on earth didn't you reply with such and such to that blighter at the back of the crowd?" he would say with a sardonic smile once I descended from the podium. He was an interesting character: a natural wit who was also a skeptic on all matters, his religious faith included. In later life he would be forced out of the Methodist church—unforgivably in my view—because of his reputed atheism. At the Bull Ring, some of Ray's lessons rubbed off on me, though it was clear my talents in such a setting would never amount to much. Still, I appreciated the bit I did learn from these experiences. There are worse things than being exposed to vocal detractors, especially for someone like me who planned to spend a considerable portion of his career speaking to audiences not so free as Bull Ring hecklers to voice their reactions in the open.

A Place in the Sun

As the years at Handsworth sped by, I was giving more and more thought to where I wanted to land after my training was done. I had little desire to stay in Britain. Not only was I restless to see some of the world, I knew that as soon as my Handsworth days were over I might be conscripted to do a stint of military service. The fact that I would be able to pass this time as a chaplain rather than a soldier was scant consolation. And so as Pat and I started to consider getting married—it took me three proposals for her to finally say yes—we spent a good deal of time discussing exactly where we might go as soon as our knot was tied.

The main impetus for our decision to emigrate to Canada was my close Handsworth friend Ray Gibbon. All through our time at the college he had been in regular correspondence with Tom Oliver, a minister from his days growing up in Redcar, Yorkshire. Oliver, who had since transferred to the United Church of Canada, lived in Vancouver. He was encouraging Ray to move to Canada once Ray had graduated. Hearing of Oliver's North American life and career, I found his suggestion appealed not just to Ray but to me as well. Each of us wrote to the Secretary of the United Church to see how we could make this move. Soon after that, life was to change for Ray. He got married while still at Handsworth, something not allowed by the Methodist Church's myriad rules for candidate ministers. As a result he paid a high price, being forced to forfeit his candidature.

So I was left alone with this dream that Ray had helped awaken, and which was then invigorated by John Stead, a businessman and Methodist layman who was vice president of the national Methodist conference. Pat and I were staying, as he was, at a Methodist holiday home named Treloyhan Manor in St. Ives, Cornwall. He had just returned from an official tour of the United Church of Canada. I was fascinated by his description of the United Church's liberalism and its tremendous need for ministers. It was clear that Canada could provide boundless opportunities

Penkridge Methodist Chapel, August 5th 1954. Lovewell family collection.

for a young candidate minister like me. When I told my parents of these plans they were highly encouraging. Not least, I was solving a major potential problem for the family, leaving the coast clear for one son, Ivan, to take over the farm. Pat, too, expressed her willingness to make this move.

However, matters were hardly uncomplicated. The clandestine plans and correspondence Ray and I had been having with United Church officials became known to Handsworth's principal, Dr. Phillip Watson. Negotiating with non-Methodists about ordination was breaking yet another rule. I was brought before a committee to investigate this aberration. I learned later that I was almost asked to leave off my studies because I was considered by the committee to be breaking faith with Methodism. But one of my mentors at the college, Dr. Charles Mitton, spoke on my behalf. It was agreed I could stay, but on condition that I paid back to the church the funds that subsidized my education. I told Father about this, and he offered to assume that debt.

A Place in the Sun

By the time of our wedding, Pat and I had cemented our plans. Five days later, after a brief honeymoon in Capelcurig, Wales, we would be heading to London Airport, in the days before it was known as Heathrow, to deposit ourselves in fresh surroundings on the other side of the Atlantic. That made the wedding itself a bittersweet occasion—the culmination of the English lives we had each led so far and the start of something completely new. With the confidence of youth, I had not the slightest doubt we were doing the right thing. (Pat, it is fair to say, was more ambivalent.) I fully intended to seek Canadian citizenship as soon as possible, letting my British passport lapse, and that is exactly what both Pat and I ended up doing. Once we had made that ocean crossing, we would have moved for good, our times in England from then on brief visits, certainly not a permanent return.

Chapter 5: Canada Bound

The Constellation droned heavily over the Atlantic when the pilot came on the intercom and announced that we had changed course and would be landing at Reykjavik. Engine trouble. *Engine trouble?* Pat and I were on our way to Gander, with arrangements having been made through the United Church's Newfoundland Conference. I had been placed as a candidate for ordination in the five-point charge of Alexander Bay, on the island's eastern coast.

The pilot's voice over the intercom had been matter of fact. "Everything is under control. We will be landing within two hours. In the meantime you will be served with a cup of tea and a biscuit." Such was British Overseas Airways' remedy for any anxious moment. Pat and I looked at each other. We didn't feel thirsty. This was another new experience since our wedding, the most frightening of them all. A five-day marriage ending on a pitch-black night in the cold Atlantic ocean with no trace after only five nights in the marriage bed? We listened silently as the plane droned on, each alone in our sombre thoughts, until we saw the welcome lights of the American military base of Keflavik which was to be our 14-hour stopover.

Our landing was noisy, bumpy, nauseating. But we were still alive and still married. We were ushered across the tarmac to a lounge with soft leather chairs and settees. Here we were able to rest for a few hours. At sunrise Pat and I took a walk outside to admire the lunar-looking landscape and the view of the mountains and large bay that separated us from the town of Reykjavik. Yes, we really had started a new life.

A Place in the Sun

Alexander Bay. "Glovertown Black and White" © Zach Bonnell.

On our return we were taken to the base's mess hall, where breakfast was being served to hundreds of American military personnel. A space had been set aside for the plane's passengers and we joined the queue to get our breakfast, buffet style. What a breakfast. Orange juice, grapefruit juice, tomato juice, eggs any style, bacon, toast, coffee, pancakes, syrup, even sweet rolls. Only a few hours before we had left a country still on rationing and here was unimaginable abundance, with a few dishes no sane English person would contemplate for breakfast. We were asked at every stop at the counter how much we wanted. Was this the New World extravagance we'd heard of for so long and which I'd glimpsed when the American servicemen came to our home for meals? Maybe Newfoundland would be like this as well.

We climbed back in the same plane that afternoon, the rest of the trip thankfully uneventful. Luckily we were expected. Charlie Freake, the minister at Gander, was on holiday but had arranged with Gordon Easton, a law student from Glovertown who had a summer job with Trans Canada Airlines, to greet us. Gordon was on duty and couldn't devote much time to us. We had questions galore that would have to be answered later. Were there any shops in Glovertown? What was the manse like? Was it as skimpy in furnishings as the letters from our Newfoundland contact Dr. Maxwell Dawe seemed to suggest? What about the train? We had tickets but would we need to reserve our seats? We asked these questions and Gordon appeared somewhat puzzled.

The train was due to leave at 7 pm but had been delayed, so we waited at the station for over an hour. When we arrived, the waiting room was empty, but as time went on people poured in until there was standing room only. No. We couldn't reserve seats unless we were travelling first class and that meant a sleeper. It was a Friday night and many were returning to their settlements for the weekend. A large group of lumberjacks came in, rough looking types, and to our amazement went straight for the washrooms, not just the men's but the ladies' as well. Pat remarked she was glad she wasn't in there at the time—we might have been on the next plane back to civilization.

The train rolled, bumped and clanked through the night, our attempts to see the landscape unsuccessful. In places we were vaguely aware of going through an unending forest of scrubby trees. We passed the shores of a few bodies of water, one very large which we later learned was Gander Lake. We disembarked at the isolated railway station at Alexander Bay, surrounded by trees, and felt very lost. Which way to go? Who would pick us up? Out of the night, through the engine's steam and smoke, a thin, short man confidently burst on us. He seemed to know who we were. We must have looked very English and lost. "Reverend (In spite of the fact that I was not yet ordained, this would be my title from now on except from fellow ministers who understood the finer meanings of address) and Mrs. Lovewell?" "Yes." "I'm Caleb and I have the taxi service in Glovertown." There were other taxi owners, but not as far as Caleb was concerned. He would have a power over us yet to be discovered. In the tone of his voice at that first moment of introduction it was already there: we were expected to heel on command.

We followed him to a huge American car, deposited our cases into the trunk and began our bumpy ride along a gravel road into the darkness. On the way Caleb attempted to tell us all we needed to know for our new life: Glovertown's various amenities, as few as they were, and some of the key people we would soon meet. He didn't stop talking until we arrived. "Reverend, our parsonage," he said as the car stopped. "Third one in five years. First one burned by a forest fire. Wonderful bad. Lost mine as well. You'll see my new place in the morning—the big one just down there," pointing into the blackness. "Got the new parsonage built and even put the furnishings in. That burned down too. Wonderful strange how it caught fire. Had to work hard to build this one. Not finished yet." We got out of the car while he retrieved our cases and led us to the door. "Any time you need a drive, call me. The big house just down there." Again he pointed into the darkness.

The parsonage was full of members of the Ladies' Aid silently waiting to welcome us. There was food galore and a kettle boiling in the kitchen. They were silent until we spoke. The black wood range was the first thing Pat commented on. "I haven't seen one like that before." Those words were to be repeated, at least to each other, for weeks to come. For us this really was a new found land and its strangeness from the life we had been used to was now fully upon us. The ladies were quiet, listening to everything we said. We were under scrutiny. We made conversation and our search for things to talk about must have made them more self-conscious than ever. The new minister and his wife would be carefully watched and listened to for some time to come.

The pastoral charge of Alexander Bay had asked for another minister, Wallace Baker, who was newly ordained, and he appears to have wanted to go. But for whatever reason the settlement committee did not place him there. Al LeGrow, a candidate for the ministry, had been filling in that summer until we came. He would stay on for a few days to see us settled. He saved us many blunders and much embarrassment with his knowledge of the place and the differences of culture that separated us from our new surroundings.

After what seemed like forever, the ladies departed and we were left at the parsonage with Al and his wife Mildred. After a brief tour of the bare house, we went to our bedroom to rest from the experiences of the past few days that had our heads spinning with bewilderment, excitement, fear, hope and the first flush of married bliss.

The bed had a brown tubular head and foot bars. On each side an orange box stood on its end covered with a small plastic mat. These were the bedside tables. Except for this furniture and the sheets and blankets on the bed, the room was bare, the floor finished with a flowered plastic that resembled linoleum.

The bathroom was incomplete, but did have the necessary equipment: toilet, hand bowl and bath. It was the bare wood at the head of the bath that gave it an unfinished look. For some reason the carpenter had left things incomplete, either from lack of materials or interest, or because he had just forgotten to return. Parts of the walls were painted, other parts overlooked. We learned later that with voluntary labour many jobs around the church and in the schools were left up to somebody to finish— and that somebody never turned up.

The night was spent in our blissful state of honeymoon—sleeping together was the most wonderful experience to land on my doorstep. We were awake early and eager to see what Glovertown looked like. Out of the bedroom window was Alexander Bay surrounded by low wooded hills. To the left was a wharf and small shipbuilding yard, to the right a large house with a number of cars and trucks outside—Caleb's place. On the opposite side of the road towards the shore was another large house. We would soon get to know Cyril and Shirley Goodyear, the local Mountie and his wife. We breathed in the cool morning air through the window and began to feel a little homesick. This was our new home and it was a long way from home.

Al and Mildred rose at about the same time as we did and made breakfast for us. They then took us on a quick tour. We were introduced to the store owners and told by Al that it would be wise to get a little from each store owned by a congregation member. We didn't understand the full import of this until later, and the wisdom of that advice came back to us again and again. To buy everything from one store would have undermined my ministry amongst the rest of the storekeepers. I learned how important it is to tread carefully when starting a ministry. Once established and accepted, liberties can be taken, but not at first. This applies to all beginning ministries, especially the rural ones.

Al also took me on rounds to meet some of the key people of the church: two Glovertown store owners named Naboth Sweetapple and Eli Arnold; Heber Arnold, who worked in Eli's store; and three lumber merchants. Two of them, Harry LeDrew and Bill Janes, lived in Glovertown. Bill, with whom I would later become close, was a wealthy sawmill owner and was perhaps the most central person in the charge. The third, Robert Powell, lived in Happy Adventure, twenty miles from Glovertown. Later on Pat and I would stay with his family during our monthly visits to Happy Adventure whenever the weather forced us to spend the night.

The first Sunday dawned with apprehension. Early morning clouds hung low over the waters of Alexander Bay. This was the day to be introduced to two of the five congregations: Glovertown Central and Traytown. Glovertown South, Happy Adventure and Saunder's Cove would be visited over the following three weeks. Happy Adventure would be for the whole day once a month, Saunder's Cove once a month but for an afternoon service. I was hoping that our marriage, our emigration to Canada, and my pending ordination into the ministry of the United Church would become a happy adventure for both of us—but at the beginning of that day it felt anything but happy or adventurous.

Waiting in the vestry was more painful than entering the pulpit. Robert Parsons was with us. He was a logger and a fisherman, depending on the season. There was no hint of a smile on his face. He was wary and suspicious, even with Al who was a fellow Newfoundlander whom he had known for a couple of months. He had nothing to say, but his demeanour spoke loudly. Al did the talking but that simply made this dour man all the more sullen. I knew that we would have to discover each other slowly. The opportunity would come tragically before the end of the summer when his daughter was killed in a freak accident while she was playing.

Each church, except Traytown, had the odour of lacquer, which had been liberally applied to the pews and floors. Even today freshly painted varnish still wafts memories of those innocent days in the summer and fall of 1954: frantically visiting and preaching, in the style I had been taught at Handsworth, constantly driven by a hunger for acceptance by those I was meeting.

I can't remember the service at Glovertown Central that morning, but I do recall Traytown's that afternoon. The church was an old wooden building which stood on a rocky knoll above the road and overlooked the inlet. There was a small pedal harmonium, pot-belly stove, foot-worn pine floor and ancient pews that looked as though they'd been made for some other sanctuary, placed here for the time being, then for want of anything better never removed.

One of the congregation members, Heber Arnold, came to Glovertown to fetch us in his red Fargo truck. He had two tall black wooden arm chairs placed in the box of the truck facing the cab. After he drove up to the parsonage, he assisted Pat and me onto the box where he encouraged us to sit on the chairs "so you can see well." The clouds had cleared and the sun was shining. He drove us along the dusty road. Sitting bolt upright, the two of us were seen, though there were no people standing by the side of the road. The town's inhabitants obviously expected us. They peered through curtained windows as though they had been concentrating on something else and we happened to pass through their line of vision.

At the church, the congregation had gathered and were silent on our entry. They sat looking straight ahead and waited until we passed them in the aisle and then turned their heads to catch their first glimpse of this young preacher fresh from foreign shores, his wife in tow. Pat sat at the front and I went to the pulpit. But what I said or did is now lost to me.

What I do remember well is an issue that arose about my clerical collar. In the Methodist Church, we wore the collar whenever preaching as student ministers. I automatically did that in Glovertown and was unaware until after ordination that in the United Church this was a no-no—clericals were a sign of ordination. This was not a concern to the people of the churches where I was preaching—it was, however, a great concern to fellow ministers and lay preachers. What conversations that must have sparked at Presbytery meetings.

Before Al and Mildred left to return to Mount Allison so Al could continue his studies, they introduced us to Cyril and Shirley Goodyear, who would become close friends and help us through our homesickness. They in turn introduced us to Ralph and Jean Belbin. Ralph was the local welfare officer, and Ralph and Jean where members of Glovertown Central. Cyril and Shirley never attended church. To have close friends on the inside and outside was a blessing. Both couples spoke freely to us about situations from their perspectives and I could share with one or the other, depending on my need to express myself or to sound them out.

The second Sunday morning I had Glovertown South scheduled for a service. The plan of services for a month had been left on my desk in my small so-called office in the parsonage. I had studied it well: one of my nightmares was not turning up when expected. We arrived at the church, and yes we were expected. We were met on the front steps about thirty minutes beforehand by Alphonse House, a happy, smiling man with a gnarled face and bowed legs. He was not as tall as Pat and welcomed us with his large hairy-backed hand. He sensed our mood, and with a fatherly warmth led us into the church that he dearly loved. After explaining the details of the service and the expectations of the congregation he took me into the lacquered, white-walled vestry. Pat was alone in the pews and had time to brood. The air was filled with the sound of pealing bells and the twitter of birds. I looked out the vestry window at the unending forest of evergreens and felt my throat tighten.

I heard the people arriving. These were from a Methodist heritage. At least we had something in common. The time came for me to step into the sanctuary and begin the service. No introductions. This had been the case in the previous two services. I must have been extremely nervous on the first Sunday, especially for the first service, because I do not remember the service or any of my feelings—the second service is less hazy but this one stands out in my mind. The first hymn was "O for a thousand tongues to sing" sung to the Winchester Old tune, which Pat and I associated with "While shepherds watch their flocks by night." I looked down at Pat. Her eyes were watering and I became aware of a solid lump in my throat—I fought back the tears. That was the beginning of our feeling so far from home. I glanced through the window and there were those interminable scrubby firs broken only by lakes and bare-rocked hills. The view from the chapel windows in Norfolk was of fields, lanes, cottages…also unending, but how invitingly unending. From that moment, we lost our appetites; our nights were punctuated with weeping, for Pat very openly, but for me, crying inside. The long heartache of missing family, village and country had broken out and could not be covered up any more and would last for me, with diminishing intensity, for the next five years.

The longing to become, and the being, the anticipation and the arrival are very different—so very different. If only I had realized that it would take a lifetime of learning to become what I then felt I had been called to be and assumed I could become straight away. The training for ministry is actually being a minister. If by one's retirement one has finally learned how not to minister then that is the best qualification to the ministry.

Unfortunately in 1954 that was of little help. I had no background or education for the ministry in the United Church of Canada, and no grounding for life in an isolated Newfoundland outport. My training was in preaching and visiting in an English Methodist rural setting. Since the United Church in Newfoundland had a Methodist history, and I interpreted Alexander Bay as being rural, I eagerly set about implementing my recently acquired skills. But there had been painfully little training in pastoral administration, personal time management or how to explore and relate to environments other those found in the English Methodist church. On top of all that I had little understanding of myself, my feelings, my motivations, my reactions, the ways I related to others. I had brought everything with me to this new situation including the debris of my past, and I didn't know how to turn that into fertilizer for present and future experiences, into creative energy, or into helpful reference points. And now the pressure was on. I had five churches to pastor, administer, lead, and hundreds of people to relate to—these were the expectations placed on me by the system, and by myself. I had my untried skills to test as well as to live with and a newly wedded wife. I stumbled into the situation with Pat as my only soul-support—together we would have to find our way.

I preached the way I had been preached to for years in the chapel at Shotesham, but somehow it did not ring true to me. My sermons came back across the attentive but suspicious pews, echoing hollowness. Mondays became my day of depression, worrying over the things I had said from the pulpit and longing for reassurance that it had been a wonderful performance. I did not know how to speak to the heart of these people, because I had no heart for them as persons. They were strangers and I had landed on their shores and had to make my own maps of their islands and of the waters that separated them from each other, and that separated them from me.

Not that Pat and I were completely bereft. Both of us by temperament are enthusiastic people, we laughed easily and each of us had long since learned how to reach out in friendly ways, and of course we had each other. Pat soon acquired a job. At that time, only five years after Newfoundland joined the rest of Canada, there were very few trained teachers in the province, particularly in out-of-the-way places such as Alexander Bay, with schools split up by denominations into seven independently governed systems. We had gone into St. John's soon after our arrival to buy a car, and Pat took advantage of that trip to set up a meeting with the United Church's school superintendent Dr. Ira Curtis. From a well-established Newfoundland family, Dr. Curtis was very aware of his position. He asked Pat how many years of training and experience she had. Pat replied three years of training and four of experience. "We can't recognize that," was his only response, so she started teaching at basic pay.[1]

Her position was in a one-room school in Glovertown North, with students from grades one to eight. A wooden building, like all others in the community, it was heated by a wood stove set in the centre of the single classroom. She started teaching that very

---

1 There was a happy end to this story. Years later, when we lived in St. John's, this oversight was rectified by a neighbour of ours, a Newfoundland judge. Pat was again teaching in the United Church system. Without any prompting from us, our neighbour had looked up her pay. Seeing how low it was, he insisted to the educational authorities that this be changed. To our delight not only was her pay immediately raised, but she received full back pay as well. Such were the ways of Newfoundland bureaucracy at that time.

first September, which allowed her an independent role in addition to her informal position as minister's wife.

For Pat, this was a return to a former occupation, given that in the years immediately prior to our marriage she had trained as a nurse. But the shift from English to Newfoundland schools was a refreshing change. She found her new pupils to be warm and cooperative. And they were keen to learn. For her this experience was by and large a rewarding one—something for which I was extremely grateful.

Christmas at the Goodyears' in Glovertown. Lovewell family collection.

Meanwhile, I gradually grew accustomed to these new surroundings and the demands being placed on a minister and his wife in pastoral life. With time, Pat and I grew particularly close with Bill Janes and his wife Margaret. They exhibited a refreshing honesty in terms of these expectations that helped me in immeasurable ways. I visited a great deal, and Pat and I took advantage of the numerous invitations we received to be entertained at many homes. On these occasions we were introduced to Newfoundland fish and meat dishes, both so different from what we were used to, and tremendous quantities of freshly baked homemade bread. The local storytellers were waiting for a fresh audience for their tall tales and we knew how to listen. We were carried at first by our latent warmth and the responsive sympathy, if not compassion, of a number of caring people, a few of whom saw and understood what we did not see and understand.

David E. Lovewell

Pat outside the Humbermouth Manse with Mark. Lovewell family collection.

But it would take longer than the two years we stayed in Alexander Bay for us to adapt to Newfoundlanders' ways, as the seas of their honesty washed up on to our rocky beaches, their humour and the ebb and flow of their tenderness re-contouring our insular English Methodism.

My own disquiet exhibited itself in continued restlessness of the sort that had brought me to Newfoundland to begin with. In the two decades after our initial departure from England, we moved a total of seven times, first to two other Newfoundland charges, next beyond Canada's borders, then back to Newfoundland and finally to Alberta. In 1956 we left for a part of Newfoundland far different from Alexander Bay in scenery and terrain. Our new home was in a mountainous region near what has become a major tourist attraction—the now famous fjords of Gros Morne and its national park. Humbermouth is a suburb of Corner Brook, Newfoundland's second-largest city. Back then it was an industrial town, its inhabitants' livelihoods tied to Corner Brook's lumber and paper industries and the mining of gyp rock. We were part of a relatively large community in a pastoral charge with two churches and, when compared with Glovertown, much more closely linked with the outside world.

Corner Brook's paper mill was owned by a British firm named Bowater's, so there was a greater English presence as well. Pat took up teaching again, and both of us found plenty to do in our jobs, she with a bigger school and I with a larger congregation.

A Place in the Sun

For both of us, acclimatization to North American life now began in earnest. Our next move in 1959 was just down the street, to First United in the centre of Corner Brook. I was the Christian Education minister, while Pat, besides teaching adult education, filled in as interim church organist and choir director. The manse was a Bowater's-built house on one of the main avenues of the city, and First United's congregation included not just factory workers but many of the company's managers as well. When Pat's relatives visited one Christmas, we were able to give them a tour of Sir Eric Bowater's house at Strawberry Hill, thanks to its housekeepers who were part of the congregation. Filled with Meissen china and imported English furniture, it was a bizarre sight in the hard-scraping Newfoundland we had come to know.

A stroll in Corner Brook. Lovewell family collection.

With the arrival of the 1960s, restlessness hit me again. I initiated what was to be a significant change in our lives when I accepted a position at the Port Royal charge in Bermuda. At that time the Methodist churches on the island were the only ones outside Canada, with the exception of the overseas missions, to employ United Church clergy. In June 1961, by way of Washington D.C. where Pat's sister and brother-in-law were living, we left cold and rainy Corner Brook for an idyllic spot in a subtropical paradise. Certainly that was the way our children Mark and Rachael viewed the event. For Pat and me, too, Bermuda was refreshingly exotic, and filled with a host of comforting reminders of Britain, then as now the island's colonial overseer.

Hosting a Church Social at the Manse. Lovewell family collection.

The Port Royal charge encompassed three very different churches. The main one, Emmanuel, boasted a building that is still a mainstay of tourist postcards: a white-roofed sanctuary in the classic island style. Its congregation combined long-time island families both black and white, newer Portuguese arrivals, mostly from the Azores, and, given the church's close proximity to the island's US naval base, a smattering of American servicemen and their families. This was a time just before the civil rights movement came to Bermuda. Race relations were improving but still grounded in colonial prejudices. That was a challenge, something that took up much of my time and energy. Pat made her own contribution to the gradually shifting tide by becoming a teacher in one of the island's all-black schools—rather rare then. The second church was all-black, made up of old Bermudian families and immigrants from the West Indies. Given the congregation's informality, warmth and strong English Methodist background, I found I

Preaching at Emmanuel. Lovewell family collection.

related with them easily. The third church was distinct yet again. Situated on Bermuda's Royal Navy base, its small congregation included naval personnel and locals who worked and lived there. But despite this widely dispersed charge, I discovered that demands on ministers in Bermuda were far from excessive. For the first time since my youth I had significant time for free reading, which allowed me to expand my horizons in fresh and interesting ways.

One author whose ideas especially resonated in these years was Jewish humanist philosopher Erich Fromm. He had left Germany for North America in the 1930s, wrote a wartime book on the rise of fascism, *Escape from Freedom*, which brought him fame, and then published an international bestseller called *The Art of Loving*. Both these books affected me deeply. I had come to know Fromm's work through a liberal American journal, *Christian Century*, which I subscribed to at the time. Fromm was not religious himself, but the fact that his thinking was so imbued with his Jewish roots added to his appeal, given my own strong empathy with Jewish thinking, no doubt influenced by my father's views. It was partly due to my reading of Fromm's books, as well as those of several other liberal-minded authors, that I found myself questioning aspects of my faith and wondering whether I should stay in the ministry.

This had little practical effect in Bermuda. Given the paradise-like nature of our lives there it was easy to lay such doubts aside. But in 1965 we moved back to Newfoundland so that I

With Rachael in a friends' Bermuda garden. Lovewell family collection.

could serve a six-month stint at Gower Street United, a large downtown church in St. John's. Then these questions did come to the fore. At the end of that half year I was called again within St. John's to Cochrane Street United. Though with a smaller congregation than Gower, Cochrane included a good number of active politicians and other well-known figures in Newfoundland society. Both Joey Smallwood, then the province's premier, and John Crosbie, his long-time political sparring partner and later a federal cabinet minister, were members of the congregation, as were Cluny Macpherson, a man who had made a name for himself as the inventor of a World War I gas mask, and his son Campbell, at that time Newfoundland's lieutenant governor.

Cochrane Street provided a different set of opportunities and challenges than any church I had served at before. Smallwood himself was a classic Newfoundland character. Though he never attended Cochrane, we did have a chance to interact with him. One Christmas, when Pat's parents were visiting us in St. John's, I thought they would enjoy meeting Smallwood. So all of us bundled into our Chevrolet Bel Air and drove to his large house which was a good distance from the city. I knocked unannounced at the door, quickly explaining who I was. Though Smallwood and I had never met, he was quite happy to invite us inside. Directing his comments to our English visitors, he proceeded to keep us all spellbound with an hour-long monologue on Newfoundland politics and history. He stopped only once when he momentarily forgot the name of a well-known figure from the past, and asked our son Mark if he could help remind him.

Restaurant dinner in St. John's. Lovewell family collection.

It was good of Smallwood, with all the demands on his time, to drop everything to chat to us that day, but his was not the only case of memorable kindness. Indeed the generosity of congregation members could take extravagant forms. One day, for example, I happened to mention to Campbell Macpherson that Pat, I and family were spending our summer vacation at Expo 67 in Montreal. A few days later, Campbell's chauffeur and limousine arrived unannounced at our manse door with a cheque "to be used to dine at the Czech pavilion." On another occasion, after I preached a sermon entitled "Joy," the same chauffeur appeared again, this time with a bottle of expensive perfume direct from Paris with the brand name Joy for Pat.

Such snippets of Newfoundland warmth were part of what was to be our last experience living in that province. Early in 1969 I accepted a call from Gaetz United Church in the Albertan city of Red Deer to be a youth minister. It was a major move. In January of that year, in the midst of a bitterly cold winter, the entire family took our Bel Air, tent trailer in tow, across the continent. Maybe because of our Newfoundland and Labrador license plates, we garnered more than our share of comment. I'll never forget the observation of one gas attendant as we stopped at his station after a particularly frigid night in a motel on the American prairie. Pointing at the tent trailer he said, "Must've been cold." Not wishing to spoil his perception of Newfoundland hardiness, I nodded. "Sure was."

Gaetz proved to be an interesting charge, and our time there was pivotal for me in several ways. While at Cochrane, my questioning had led me to muse for a short period about shifting my career into social work. The fresh vistas of the Canadian West somehow caused such musings to pass. The congregation at Gaetz was especially welcoming, and I found myself working with a senior minister with a colourful background. A larger than life figure named Ed Oldring, he had been a Canadian fighter pilot during the war. His distinctive religious views were encapsulated in a book he was preparing to write while at Gaetz. Its title, *I Walk and Talk with Angels,* gives a good indication of his thinking. Despite our theological differences, he and I got along well. Pat and I were also part of a bible study group that provided considerable spiritual stimulation. Amongst its members, I found I could share my questioning and drew renewed inspiration and support.

In many ways, Gaetz was transitional for both Pat and me. We did not stay in Red Deer all that long, but in our three and a half years there we became deeply involved in the spiritual life of Gaetz, and I was very appreciative of the way in which church members helped me revitalize my vocation. When we did move it was to a church that was the apex of my ministry: St. Andrew's in Calgary. At my very first meeting with the church's pastoral relations committee, I remember being struck by the enthusiasm of its members and attracted by their keenness to have me accept their call. Both Pat and I were to continue to experience that refreshing enthusiasm during the next 13 years.

In retrospect that period—the late 1970s and early to mid-1980s—was a propitious time to be a minister in the booming southwest region of Calgary. Especially during the early part of my ministry there the city was growing by leaps and bounds, with a continuing influx of families. The dynamism of the city in those days was brought home to me by the number of couples who sought out the church, with its distinctively modern sanctuary, as a wedding venue. Sometimes I would officiate at as many as seven ceremonies on a Saturday, not to mention three services the next morning on Sunday.

St. Andrew's United, Calgary.
© Bob Schroeder.

It was gratifying to see the growth in the congregation during those years. The number that has stayed with me is 1400 families. But not all was expansion and prosperity. Many in the congregation felt the rough economic times that faced Alberta in the early 1980s, during a bad slump in the oil business, and I remember the enthusiasm with which St. Andrew's members reached out to help those in difficulty. Our friends there also showed exceptional support to our family. Their openness and informality—very much in keeping with the city and province in which the church was situated—is my most enduring memory of what in retrospect seem like golden years.

But golden years must come to an end, and by the mid-1980s the demands of a large congregation were beginning to tell, though my enthusiasm was undimmed. The restlessness I had experienced several times in the past returned, and I began seriously considering another move—this one, I realized, likely to be

*At a St. Andrew's event.
Lovewell family collection.*

the last of my career. I had been receiving periodic invitations to move to other churches, but until 1986 had turned down each one. At this point I made a conscious switch, deciding to follow up on the next prospective call. So when First United Church, a large and well-established congregation in downtown Victoria, came knocking, I was ready. Pat and I were already familiar with Victoria: it had been the western-most stop on several of our summer holidays and we were both drawn by the prospect of living in a milder climate on the beautiful Pacific coast. We moved in the fall of that year. By West Coast standards, First United had a strong sense of its own history. The congregation included a large proportion of educated professionals, many of them retired. Though the influence of the church's past loomed larger than it had in other charges I served in, we received a warm welcome, and church members were very gracious when just three years later I announced my intention to take early retirement, having reached the age of 60.

Chapter 6: My Final Sermon

Although I can hardly hear the alarm, it wakes me as it does every morning. The instruction pamphlet must name the tune playing in my sleepy ear every day at 6 am from my bedside table, but I have long since lost the pamphlet, and after two years I haven't been able to unravel the tangle of notes scrambled by the timepiece's maker into the electronic maze of its silicon chip.

It's Sunday morning and I am being awakened to prepare to stand in the pulpit once again and claim to speak about another maker's intention, as if I knew the tunes, let alone the words, that angels sing. Such waking realization brings again the twinge that had been speaking to me with a slowly increasing volume over latter years, "What audacity to stand and say to people in the pews, 'This is the word of the Lord.'"

On this particular Sunday, after the alarm dutifully renders its song, my right hand shoots out from under the sheets and gropes for the radio for my wake-up dose of CBC News. The familiar voice informs me: "A big change is taking place this weekend...." My hazy mind is suddenly snapped into full consciousness. That's me: today marks my big change. I hear no more of the news. It plays as music does, background for my ruminating. This is my last Sunday as minister at First United Church, and my last sermon as a minister.

As I labour over my shaving, I realize that I have used the same blade a number of times and it is losing its sharpness. I give my face another brush of lather and I think of my arrival in Glovertown in August 1954, keen, enthusiastic, ready to cut my own swath. Have I lost that original edge over the years? Have my efforts been just a repeated cosmetic job with no radical effects,

First United Church, Victoria.
Lovewell family collection.

even on me? My attention is momentarily deflected by these recurring nagging questions and I nick the edge of my lip at the corner of my mouth, the final application of lather stained red.

I shower, clean my teeth, comb my hair and dress. In the mirror I look presentable. The broken skin has quickly clotted and is quite unnoticeable to anybody else. I can step out into the day reasonably assured until looking at myself in tomorrow's mirror before the scraping, washing and grooming begins again. On this Sunday I have one final job to do, one final word to speak, and I have to give it all my attention from now until the service is over.

Sunday morning breakfast is quiet as usual. Since I use no notes I have to keep going through what I am to say. Pat understands this. She drives me to First United just after 7. My first half hour is spent walking around the sanctuary talking to God—yes, talking to God as Mother taught me to do as a child. I know of no other way to respond to the words of Jesus, "Watch and pray!" Most mornings I engage in this simple act of telling God all those things that are on my mind, remembering my family first and then the people I will be dealing with. On Sundays I think of those who will be sitting in the pews listening to me. But how do I pray today? This is the end of a way of life and I'm not quite sure how tomorrow is going to turn out, or all the other unstructured tomorrows that will follow. "God, you called me once to do something: take on a ministry of word and sacrament and pastoral care. It was once clear and unquestionable. But on this last Sunday I don't have a feeling of accomplishment, of a calling fulfilled. I do, however, have a feeling that there are other things for me to do and I'm not sure yet what they are. I'll have to leave that in your hands for now and give myself some time." And then I remember again Jesus's words: "Watch and pray!" Yes, that's what I'll have to do to ensure that my resolve does not become sporadic, as it has at earlier points in my ministry and faith experience.

I have to stop this. I've got to get down to what I will say later. There has always been the necessity to publish a sermon title every week, a practice I have never felt comfortable with. This Saturday's newspaper title was "I believe this, but it may be wrong."

Throughout my 43 years of preaching I have used many words to propound a mélange of vaguely consistent ideas, though as I look back I can't help but shudder at times at all I've said. At one point in my ministry in the early 1970s, when I moved to St. Andrew's from Gaetz in Red Deer, I had the same feeling. I took all my sermons from the file folder and threw them on the fire. Whether there will be another such burning I can't tell at this point, but I feel like doing it. I am conscious of having talked about things of which I know so little and probably appeared to know so much. And all the time the form of service which we use names the sermon as "The Word" as if what I impart is somehow straight from the Lord. But I am becoming aware this Sunday that my beliefs are just starting to come into focus, slowly, tentatively at the end of my ministry. They have been whittled down to trusting in the God of grace, and all I can say now is that I am endeavouring to trust God as I trusted my mother and father all those years ago back in Shotesham. That is really all I can say and that doesn't take long, so maybe that is all that I should ever say.

Much of what I've spoken from the pulpit has not been well thought out. On the rare occasions when it was, it was only my opinion—and in that I may have been totally wrong. I must somehow relay that message, hence today's title. I continue to walk around the pews changing, adding, taking away. This is the way

David E. Lovewell

Preparing...
Lovewell family collection.

I have been taught to refine a sermon so that it is fresh in my mind for what appears to be an impromptu delivery. And it is only after the sermon is delivered that it will be committed to paper by the church secretary from the live recording of the service so I can edit it for its final delivery to congregation members unable to attend church.

Cullen, the caretaker, comes into the church and I know it is time to prepare for the congregation's arrival. He has grown used to my Sunday morning wanderings and never says a word except a quick hello. As he arranges the flowers for the service and brings the glass of water to the pulpit, he looks at me, holding up the glass and says, "Will you need this or a Kleenex this morning?"

Unbeknownst to him he is pointing to the missing part of my ministry. As I look back over the years, one thing has been absent—tears, my tears. I'm sure I have felt a measure of compassion many times, but has the compassion come out of my heart or my head? The truth hits me—my ministry has been a tearless ministry. I've done everything but weep. Is that where I have erred? Maybe the sermon should have been entitled "I have not wept and that has been my shortfall." But the past cannot be changed.

The service begins in the same way as the Sunday before and the Sunday before that. The scripture readings are assigned by the lectionary, but I have selected the hymns that best sum up what I will be saying and where I feel the congregation will be that morning. I go through the whole service as a performer who has thoroughly rehearsed everything, and even though it is my last Sunday I don't feel a lump in my throat. A kind of numbness maybe, a mixture of nervousness and looking forward to a whole new way of life.

After the service there are refreshments and a presentation in the church hall. I find it awkward saying so many goodbyes. Darleen, one of the church secretaries, comes up and thanks me: "That was a good sermon, but I may be wrong!" At least one person heard me.

Then come speeches and a presentation of a painting by a Vancouver Island artist. It portrays an eagle hovering a few feet above the broken trunk of an old mountain oak. A lonely eagle high up amongst the peaks. A soaring eagle with a view of the valley and distant ranges. An eagle coming in for a landing on an exposed oak whose topmost branches have been broken by lightning or wind, to rest in preparation for its next flight. An eagle being itself on one of its journeys and entering fully into its present with watchful eye, powerful reflexes and an unconscious drive for survival. After all, as well as wings for soaring the eagle has talons, claws and an incisive beak. As I stare at my gift for a brief moment I realize I am peering into another mirror, again naked, but looking inside. What I have been given to mark the end of my formal ministry and the beginning of my new life is a picture of promise that immediately reminds me of some verses from Isaiah, verses I have loved ever since first hearing them on my father's knee so many decades ago:

> *They who wait for the Lord shall renew their strength,*
> *They shall mount up with wings as eagles,*
> *They shall run and not be weary,*
> *They shall walk and not faint.*

Chapter 7: Re-Creation

Erich Fromm had something interesting to say about old age. It is a phase of life, he said, when we must face the inevitability of physical decay, but it can also be a time of mental reinvigoration, as long as we keep in mind that "recreation can become re-creation."[1] Those words have stuck with me.

Since I gave that last sermon in 1989, both Pat and I have been lucky to enjoy good health, while living in a city and a home that we love. During the quarter century that has passed since that day, I have made my own attempts at re-creation. Some of my interests have been rediscoveries from the past; others have been new. Among the rediscoveries has been my love for astronomy, which I am now able to pursue with the aid of wonderful new forms of computer technology. While I have done less telescope-gazing than in my youth, or during our time in Bermuda when thanks to a congregation member I had access to a 24-inch telescope, I have been able to gain a much fuller appreciation of the scientific marvels that infuse the night sky.

My longtime interest in poetry has also been reawakened. Through an important friendship forged in the 1990s I joined a reading circle on William Blake. I had long known and admired a few Blake poems, but my appreciation was comparatively limited. Thanks to the camaraderie provided by the reading group, as well as the publication during the 1990s of a beautiful series of facsimile editions of Blake's illustrated works, I and the other members were able to take time to study his religious poetry, as

---

[1] Quoted in Lawrence J. Friedman, *The Lives of Erich Fromm: Love's Prophet* (New York: Columbia University Press, 2013), p. 267.

A Place in the Sun

Living room view from Paramont Place. Lovewell family collection.

we tackled each line and visual detail of the accompanying paintings to gain as much as we could from his inspired, if at times highly esoteric, literary visions.

A completely new interest was genealogy, again much aided by computer resources, as I consulted online databases, as well as reaching out via genealogical websites and by email to others around the world working on family trees with links to my own. It was a project that brought its share of discoveries of the sort with which any amateur genealogist will be acquainted. Thanks to at least one

From The Echoing Green, by William Blake.

"interestingly" complicated family situation, for example, it is by no means clear what our last name should really be. On one of our visits to England, Pat and I had the chance to visit the Norfolk County records office for several days running to find as many records as we could on the Lovewell family's history. We discovered that my great grandfather William, the first of the Lovewells to move to Shotesham, had an illegitimate birth. The baptismal records include the name of his mother Elizabeth Lovewell and father William Killington, and they show that Elizabeth and William married three years later.[2]

For whatever reason William Lovewell chose to keep his mother's name—probably simply to avoid the inconvenience of undergoing a legal name change. But while his intentions can never be known, the impact of his decision is clear: it meant that for a century and a half our family has enjoyed a classic-sounding yet distinctive English surname more often found in Restoration comedies than in real life. Even today Lovewells are relatively rare—with most in the United States rather than Britain. I for one am thankful to my great grandfather for choosing as he did. Still, it does appear that this chance borrowing will soon come to an end, for by an interesting set of procreative coincidences not a single one of my great grandfather's descendants in future generations will bear Lovewell as a surname.

And just as I've delighted in discoveries about the Lovewells' past, I've had the pleasure to see much unearthed about Grove Farm, though in this case I've been nothing more than an interested bystander. In the early 1980s the farmhouse was bought by Anthony and Heather Jackson, who undertook a thoroughgoing restoration that uncovered much early detail, while they commissioned both a historical survey and documentary history

---

[2] I discovered the details of William Lovewell's 1830 birth in the parish records of the Norfolk village of Kirstead, which also record Elizabeth Lovewell's marriage in 1833 to William Killington.

A Place in the Sun

Mark visiting Grove Farm in 2014. Lovewell family collection.

of the house which, along with other much cherished mementoes of the house's past, they have kindly shared with the Lovewell family.[3] With Grove Farm's past placed in the hand of experts, it has been satisfying to learn that many of my boyish speculations about the house have finally been answered—to the extent, of course, that final answers are possible. It is highly probable that the original structure dates from the reign of Henry VIII, with major additions a century later. As the house was then passed down through six sales and multiple inheritances[4] it seems likeliest that

---

3   A. Longcroft, *Grove Farm, Shotesham All Saints: An Historical Survey* (unpublished typescript, 1994); Geoffrey I. Kelley, *Grove Farm, Shotesham All Saints: A History Based Upon Documentary Sources* (unpublished manuscript, 2000).

4   According to Kelley's history, the site of the house was likely occupied in the late medieval period, probably as freehold, and possibly by a family called Coles. John Curson probably built the original part of the structure still standing today, the property then passing to George Kett (son of Robert and grandfather of the later George Kett) in or before 1590. Later sales were by Kett heirs to a Norwich surgeon Thomas Ekins in 1732, by Ekins heirs to Benjamin Dyball a

Reliving courtship memories. Lovewell family collection.

those enigmatic words *Veritas odium parit* inscribed in the gable brickwork were placed there by the house's owner in the mid-17th century. George Kett was the great grandson of the outspoken Norfolk rebel Robert Kett, who was hanged from the walls of Norwich Castle in 1549, which leads to the natural inference that these words are a descendant's coded allusion to Kett's populist uprising—a fitting counterpoint to the legend (and it is only fair to say that the commissioned historians view it as such) of Henry Howard's birth on the farm.

While appreciating such discoveries about the past, Pat and I took every chance to enjoy the present. We were able to travel extensively. The trips with the most lasting memories were two to Australia, visiting members of my extended family who had ended up there. The reason they are in Australia is due to events in England dating back to the 1950s. My mother's sister Doris and her husband Eddy found little opportunity in post-war Norfolk. He worked in a 1950s version of a seniors' care home. The work was hard, and chances of advancement were few—something of great worry to a man with seven children. The family became Christadelphians, a religious group that used to be well known for its determination to have its adherents spread throughout the

---

Norwich gentleman in 1742, by Dyball heirs to Robert Fellowes (father of the Robert Fellowes mentioned in Chapter 1) in 1840, by Edward Fellows to George Lovewell in 1920, and by Ivan Lovewell to Anthony and Heather Jackson in 1983.

Commonwealth. That meant that my aunt and uncle were able to get official help to make the move to Australia. The family had never returned to England afterwards, so when Pat and I visited my cousins and their offspring in the 1990s it was a particularly bittersweet reunion. Because of our own experiences, both Pat and I could empathize with the family's stories of their arrival and the challenges they faced in their first home in a remote village in Western Australia. By the 1990s my cousins were scattered throughout the continent, which meant that we had many places to see, including that village where the family's Australian journey started. We couldn't help comparing their story with ours. One thing Pat and I agree on is that my aunt and uncle and their family had a harder time as they started their lives anew. It makes the successes of their children and grandchildren all that much more impressive.

As for Pat and me, our travelling days are now done. We have lived in our current home longer than either of us has lived in any other. The city of Victoria has a multitude of benefits for those in our position. Some are practical, such as the balmy climate, at least by Canadian standards, superb health care, thanks to a national medical system that still works, and a leisurely pace of life which for many family visitors from England is a reminder of the 1950s. As for Canadian visitors, the term "God's waiting room" is often used. There is one other great advantage—that so many friends from former days have also ended up in this city. Some of our most satisfying Victoria moments have been thanks to these reunions.

In line with Erich Fromm's thinking, a fully lived old age is not just a matter of having many interests, but even more importantly living in the present, something Pat admits she finds more difficult than I do. At this point in our lives, looking too much into the future is not a particularly productive pastime, although Pat and I had the pleasure of looking forward to our diamond wedding anniversary this year.

David E. Lovewell

For me, the sentiments associated with this time of life are easiest to capture in poetry. So I end these pages with a poem I wrote soon before finishing these memoirs—just in time to be included in the accompanying volume of my poetry, whose title *Evening Reflections* is the same as that of this verse:

> Evening creeps slowly
> From the fading light
> of the setting sun to the
> impending darkness
> of the inevitable night.
>
> The armchair envelopes
> in warmth before the
> flame of the flickering fire.
>
> The words in the lines of a book
> run gently past the eyes
> as the story unfolds and triggers
> the imagination in multiple
> directions.
>
> Life is gentle and soft
> as the day starts to wind down.
> Conversation breaks the silence
> as the line shouts out from the page
> and demands the attention
> of the reader's companion.
>
> There is more than the warmth of the room,
> there is the warmth of shared ideas
> that is the inspiration of future conversations
> as well as an ever deepening relationship.